D0394073

JENRETTE

JENRETTE
The Contrarian Manager

RICHARD H. JENRETTE

McGraw-Hill
New York   San Francisco   Washington, D.C.   Auckland   Bogotá
Caracas   Lisbon   London   Madrid   Mexico City   Milan
Montreal   New Delhi   San Juan   Singapore
Sydney   Tokyo   Toronto

Library of Congress Cataloging-in-Publication Data applied for.

McGraw-Hill

A Division of The **McGraw·Hill** Companies

Copyright © 1997 by Richard H. Jenrette. All rights reserved. Printed in the United States of America. Except as permitted under the United States Copyright Act of 1976, no part of this publication may be reproduced or distributed in any form or by any means, or stored in a data base or retrieval system, without the prior written permission of the publisher.

1 2 3 4 5 6 7 8 9 0   DOC/DOC   9 0 2 1 0 9 8 7

ISBN 0-07-032935-4

The sponsoring editor for this book was Philip Ruppel, the editing supervisor was Patricia V. Amoroso, and the production supervisor was Pamela A. Pelton. It was set in Fairfield by Donald Feldman of McGraw-Hill's Professional Book Group composition unit.

Printed and bound by R. R. Donnelley & Sons Company.

Photo credits appear on page ii, which constitutes an extension of the copyright page.

McGraw-Hill books are available at special quantity discounts to use as premiums and sales promotions, or for use in corporate training programs. For more information, please write to the Director of Special Sales, McGraw-Hill, 11 West 19th Street, New York, NY 10011. Or contact your local bookstore.

CONTENTS

FOREWORD

I was at once wary, energized, complimented, and most of all pleased when Dick Jenrette asked me to write an introduction to this book. Indeed, in recent months as Dick and I have shared adjoining offices in Donaldson, Lufkin & Jenrette's striking new headquarters building, giving our own interpretations to our roles as senior advisors to the firm, I have waited as the familiar Jenrette handwritten scrawl was transcribed by his ever-faithful assistant, Maria Fitzsimmons. I did not seek access to the yellow lined pages until they were transformed into the draft that has now become the tome in your hands. The wait was worth it, as I am sure you will soon discover.

My wariness stemmed from a premonition that I might be tempted to write a revisionist treatise to correct Jenrette's recitation of "history"—to set the record straight at least as far as my own recollection of the first 15 years of DLJ's existence that we shared. Such temptation has been resisted.

I was energized by the stimulus and challenge of debating—perhaps even arguing, as we did so many years ago—about elements of management style. "No Dick, a hasty decision at this point will get us in trouble. We need to think it through, sleep on it, so that we can be steady and undeterred in the implementation of what we decide. Yes Dick, I know that Aries are decisive and Geminis like to think it over...." An eternal debate!

I was complimented after all these years of going our professional separate ways, of gaining experience that might confirm or deny our earlier instincts as to management philosophy, that Dick would ask me to speak to his potential readers *before* he did—as an introduction to his book.

But above all, I was deeply pleased that I was to be given the opportunity to say a few words about my admiration and appreciation for my long-time partner and friend Dick Jenrette, the man who characterizes himself as the contrarian manager. As he notes, certain publishers have called this book a management text, perhaps a memoir, or possibly a Wall Street history. For my money Dick has, instead, through this effort shown himself to be a true teacher, and like most outstanding teachers, he has used his management career as an ongoing learning experience, first for himself, and now as a reflective guideline or template for the next generation of managers and entrepreneurs.

Whereas I would not quibble with Dick's highlighting of his contrarian nature (although I have been quick to counsel my own students that it is the *correct* contrary opinion—not just *a* contrary opinion—that makes for extraordinary investment and management success), it is my own view that the transcending lesson this unique man puts forth between the lines is the ultimate importance of his abiding interest in and support of the "human" side of his colleagues and friends. From his interest in the Zodiac signs, to the personal character implications of color preference, to his abiding care for the psyche, and interest in the professional and personal successes and travails of his associates, Dick has put his faith in the human element into the management equation. This was and is no act nor schooled technique for this courtly, competitive, highly intelligent gentleman from the South. It is in his very nature, and it is this human and humane quality that has made him such an essential ingredient in the success of two organizations he helped guide through the difficult years that both experienced.

Dick has presented his readers with reflections that, in my view, will be of immense value to any practitioner or student of management—from his observations on the power of partnership and the pitfalls of seeking to replicate oneself in selecting those for advancement, to his wholehearted endorsement of the most fundamental of DLJ's corporate goals since day one, "to have fun."

Beyond the thoughts and reflections he imparts based on the real-world experience of helping to lead and manage two major U.S. financial organizations, he has given us all a rare, candid, and hence valuable insight into the personal discipline, motivation, and values of a man who has painted a unique canvas for his own life.

Upon reflection, Dan Lufkin and my early embrace of an adage that Dick puts forth—surround yourself with people that are better and smarter than you—was nowhere more evident than in our decision at the beginning to ask Dick to join us in a voyage that started some 38 years ago.

William H. Donaldson

New York City
March 1997

PREFACE

This book grew out of a speech I gave to students at the Harvard Business School. The invitation to speak noted that I have had two very different management experiences. First was the entrepreneurial experience of starting a brand new company, Donaldson, Lufkin & Jenrette, Inc., which grew to become one of Wall Street's major investment banking powers. The second experience was a successful corporate turnaround of The Equitable Life Assurance Society, a huge mutual life insurer that had fallen on hard times. The invitation to speak said, "Tell us what lessons you learned from these two very different experiences."

That was my assignment, but I decided to add a third section on my personal philosophy in business—and life—as a bit of *lagniappe*.

The speech must have had some success. Afterwards several students remarked, "Why don't you turn this into a book?" As an old college journalism major who landed on Wall Street, I decided to try to reinstate my journalism credentials by producing this book. It is *not* ghostwritten, for better or worse.

As I looked back over the key decisions and strategies used successfully at both DLJ and Equitable, I recognized a common thread. Over and over, I acted as a contrarian—going against the conventional wisdom, following my instincts. In short, doing things differently. As a result I decided to call my book *The Contrarian Manager*.

While I had intended this book to be a management text of sorts, it immediately became apparent that there are no rules on how to be a contrarian. Contrarians tend to distrust set ways of doing things. The best way to illustrate contrarian thinking seemed to be through two case histories—DLJ and

Equitable—which show how a contrarian approach helped to overcome very formidable obstacles.

Perhaps misunderstanding the case-method approach to teaching, my publisher said to me, "Mr. Jenrette, what you have written is a memoir, not a management text." Memoir or whatever, I hope the reader will learn from my experiences.

In closing, I'd like to thank the many friends who contributed to the long and happy career I have enjoyed on Wall Street. I especially want to thank Maria Fitzsimmons, who has been my secretary for the past 20 years. In addition to putting up with all my ups and downs over the years, she painstakingly transcribed all my illegible handwriting into this book. I also want to apologize to those whose names and great deeds I have not chronicled here. I am grateful nonetheless.

Richard H. Jenrette

New York City
March 1997

JENRETTE

WHY A
CONTRARIAN VIEW?

L ong after I had decided to write this book, I came across a quote from Steve Spurrier, the highly successful football coach of the University of Florida Gators, that pretty well summarizes my point of view. "I am a little different," he told *Sports Illustrated*. "I read something once that I think is so true: If you want to be successful, you have to do it the way everybody else does it and do it a lot better—or you have to do it differently."

While I have never met Steve Spurrier, these few words perfectly make the case for a contrarian approach to management: "doing it differently." There are obvious advantages—the element of surprise, since usually no one is expecting what you are about to do. When you are pioneering something new, you are also not subject to invidious comparisons with the competition—"you're too small, too new to compete, etc." Indeed, the goal should be *not* to have any competition. You are creating your own market, your own niche where you can excel on your own terms.

It's also more fun to do things differently. Life and business should not be boring, though so many people try to make it so. At Donaldson, Lufkin & Jenrette, the investment banking and securities firm I helped found 36 years ago, our final corporate objective was "to have fun." We took a lot of kidding about that over the years, but it works and is still listed as one of the firm's corporate objectives. DLJ gets better and better—and more fun—as the years go by. That seems to be the way with Steve Spurrier's football teams.

1

Being a contrarian is not everyone's dish of tea. "To thine own self be true" is still the best advice, and if you are a very traditional, very conventional, very methodical individual there's no point in trying to make yourself over into a maverick. Go ahead and "do it the way everybody else does it and do it a lot better," which, as Steve Spurrier points out, is the usual way to succeed. But at least by reading this book, I hope you will attain a greater appreciation, and tolerance, of unconventional habits of thinking which may help improve even a traditional management style.

Similarly, while I classify myself as a contrarian by nature, I always make sure I have plenty of conventional, hard analytical thinking around to tell me why my latest brainstorm makes no sense and won't work. The key to success is that delicate balance when the forces of inertia don't squash creative contrarian thinking, but are sufficient to ensure that the idea is carefully researched and, if it is to be pursued, all the small but important details of execution and implementation have been reviewed. The good contrarian chief executive officer must recognize and appreciate the importance of the methodical, detail-oriented thinking that is essential to implementing a new approach. And when the shoe is on the other foot, i.e., the traditional management approach is in command, the CEO is well advised to have some nontraditional contrarian thinkers on hand to challenge orthodoxy. Perhaps the message is that we must try to resist the narcissistic impulse to clone ourselves. Great companies and organizations need diversity, not "group think."

How do you know if you are a contrarian? Most of us inherently know our true nature, if we stop and think about it for a while and are honest with ourselves. You can't tell a contrarian just by looking at a person. Outwardly, I've always been rather conventional and traditional—Brooks Brothers clothes (or is that now contrarian as informal "dress-down days" take over in the office?), the "right" clubs, knowing all the "right" people," etc. But deep down I know I'm a contrarian at heart and like to challenge the orthodox way of looking at things. This does not mean that we contrarians are all revolutionaries.

For example, I get just as mad as most conservatives at the preponderance of politically correct thinking on campus today. It takes a contrarian to stand up to this onslaught of political correctness, which can become absurd at times. The contrarian instinctively reacts against anything that becomes conventional wisdom.

Contrarian investing has long been a popular term on Wall Street to describe those investors who believe the conventional wisdom is always wrong, by definition, in the marketplace. Once everyone has become a believer in a particular stock or industry, or the market itself, there are no new believers or investors to come in and bid the stock—or the market—to still higher prices. There is, however, big downside risk if the conventional wisdom somehow turns out to be wrong. I suspect that over the long run, contrarian-thinking portfolio managers are better. In the short run the trend followers who caught the latest wave will always look better. Their motto is "The trend is your friend." The absence of major market sell-offs in recent years has not given the contrarian portfolio managers many opportunities to demonstrate their bravery under adversity. Trend, or so-called momentum investors, are definitely à la mode. That says to me, watch out!

In analyzing my own emotions as an investor over 40 years on Wall Street of watching the ups and downs of the stock and bond markets, I long ago concluded I was best as a contrarian investor—as contrasted to someone good at spotting a trend well after it got under way and riding it to new heights. I was always at my best when "the end of the world seems nigh," such as in 1974 and again in 1980, when interest rates soared to double-digit levels and the markets collapsed, or again when the stock market collapsed in 1987. The collapse of the real estate markets in the early 1990s also created some extraordinary buying opportunities for contrarian-minded investors. Deep in my psyche I always recall the voice of Bud Newquist, my early mentor on my first job on Wall Street at Brown Brothers Harriman & Co. During some market crisis, he observed "the worse things get, the more they will bounce back." He was a congenital long-term optimist with great faith in America's future. And so we bought heavily, and some months later the market did turn and rose with a vengeance to the benefit of our clients. This experience was one of my first lessons that *problems always create opportunities*—if we can clear our heads and look about us while everyone else is wringing their hands in despair.

If I was pretty good at catching market bottoms, I was less good on tops. I always had to fight an almost irresistible urge to get out too soon. I suppose this was the contrarian in me not wanting to follow the herd. The only thing that saved me from this impulse was the thought of paying capital gains taxes if I sold and admiration for Warren Buffett's style of investing in a few superb companies and holding those investments for the long term.

I don't really have any delusions that I am a great investor. Indeed, I don't know how even to grade myself since most of my life has been spent as a manager of people rather than in managing portfolios of stocks and bonds.

On the other hand, as a manager of people or of a company, I find I'm at my best when times are tough. This seems to be a hallmark of contrarians: We don't panic (famous last words!). And so, over the years I've developed a philosophy—and tried to inculcate it in my partners—try to find a way to turn every problem into an opportunity. You don't even have to be a contrarian to remember this. Problems *always* create opportunities.

ORIGINS OF MY MANAGEMENT PHILOSOPHY

The management philosophy—or style (probably a better term)—which I describe in this book evolved over the course of a mostly happy and prosperous 40-year career on Wall Street. It is a product of two very different experiences.

First was the very entrepreneurial experience of founding and nurturing Donaldson, Lufkin & Jenrette, Inc., a new, some say upstart, securities firm which burst on the Wall Street scene in 1960. At the time, DLJ was the first totally new securities firm since the Depression of the 1930s (a comforting thought to me as a contrarian). While start-ups are a dime a dozen today on Wall Street, the founding of DLJ by three young Harvard Business School graduates seemed totally avant-garde, and very risky, at the time. It simply wasn't done. Everything was very traditional on Wall Street, very clublike and "old school tie." There was also the lingering fear that the Depression could return once the post-World War II prosperity had run its course. Some 35 years later, DLJ now ranks among the nation's top half dozen or so investment banking firms in terms of level of profitability, underwriting activity, and overall prestige. By no means was this straight-line growth. The extended down periods in the 1970s sorely tested my contrarian instincts that things would get better. DLJ's current success came only after quite a few of these soul-testing experiences along the way. A look at the roster of firms appearing on Wall Street "tombstone" advertising of new issues of securities in 1960 will attest that this was no easy road—most of these firms are defunct. Among the major investment banking firms today, DLJ is the only one started as a totally new company in the post-World War II period.

The second defining experience for me was almost the diametric opposite—a mandate to try to turn around The Equitable Life Assurance Society, a 135-year-old giant mutual life insurance company, one of the four or five largest in the nation, depending on which definition one uses. Equitable, beset by high-cost guaranteed interest contract liabilities and too much real estate in a bad market, had fallen on hard times and was listing badly. Turning around a tradition-bound company, with more than 25,000 employees and agents and no discernible owners (as a mutual company, Equitable was nominally owned by its 2.5 million policyholders) was a totally different challenge than the DLJ experience. Yet I found many of my experiences at DLJ—especially those incurred during hard times—were the best possible preparation for what I faced in becoming chief executive officer of The Equitable.

Interestingly, the solution to the problem, or the salvation, for both companies turned out to be the same: public ownership. When privately owned DLJ shocked the New York Stock Exchange in 1970 by becoming the first New York Stock Exchange member firm to sell its shares to the public, the entire securities industry, not just DLJ, may have been saved from disaster when hard times came only a few years later. During the Arab oil embargo of 1973–1974, interest rates surged to double-digit levels, stocks and bonds collapsed, trading volume dried up, and the Securities and Exchange Commission persisted in its plan to "unfix" fixed commission rates on the NYSE (the right move but with abysmally bad timing given the other crises faced by the Street at that time). The permanent capital for the securities industry that resulted from its earlier move to public ownership certainly saved DLJ, and perhaps even far larger Merrill Lynch, which had followed DLJ into public ownership. It also marked the beginning of a massive shift in balance of power—away from the banks and insurance companies—toward the securities and mutual funds industries over the next 25 years. Since DLJ broke the barrier to public ownership in 1970, the securities industry's capital has grown at a 20 percent annual rate.

The key to solving Equitable's problems was not dissimilar, and equally contrarian. First and foremost, we had to get rid of the straightjacket of being a mutual, i.e., a company solely owned by its policyholders. This form, which seemed archaic to me—hardly a popular view at the time—prohibited the company (and all other mutuals) from accessing the capital markets to raise badly needed new equity capital to finance growth and offset operating losses that had eroded Equitable's capital position. This decision to demutualize The Equitable, undertaken in 1990, 20 years after DLJ's pioneering move to public ownership, represented by far the largest demutualization in the history of the United States.

As was the case with DLJ breaking the barrier to public ownership, Equitable's decision to demutualize and go public shocked the staid mutual life insurance industry (which pleased me as a contrarian). Cynics said demutualization would take five years to complete or couldn't be done at all. In fact, it took just over two years of blood, sweat, and tears—racing against the clock before the wolves could close in, as they did on a number of large insurance companies such as Executive Life and Mutual Benefit Life. Relief came just in time, in the form of a $1 billion capital infusion from AXA, the large French insurer headed by an entrepreneurial Frenchman, Claude Bébéar, who immediately became our Lafayette in Equitable's hour of need. Since those harrowing days in the early 1990s, Equitable has streamlined its operations and used its new access to the capital markets to raise nearly $3 billion of new capital, including equity and debt. The company is again solidly profitable (aftertax operating profits of nearly $500 million in 1996 contrasted with losses of several hundred million annually in the early 1990s).

I might add parenthetically that I am surprised that other mutual life insurers have not followed Equitable's lead in shifting to public ownership. The mutuals are lagging badly in public perception, sales, and growth of capital vis-à-vis other financial institutions. The current strong capital markets represent a golden opportunity to break out of the mutual straightjacket, to the benefit of the policyholders and the long-term financial viability of the companies.

But this is *not* intended to be a book about how DLJ and its former money management arm Alliance Capital together grew from nothing in 1960 to pretax earnings, between them, of $667 million in 1996 with more than $200 billion of assets under management, or how Equitable regained its stature as an industry leader after its perilous close call. Rather this is a book about "lessons learned" and the contrarian management style which I evolved to cope with both the problems and opportunities that were faced along the way in these two diverse experiences. In writing this book, I obviously believe there is something in this experience that will be valuable to other managers, bearing in mind that each of us is different and what worked for me might be inappropriate or ineffective for another person of different temperament.

Since I am a product of the Harvard Business School (Class of 1957) and its famous (although sometimes derided) case method of teaching, it comes natural to me to use the case method in this book to illustrate the lessons I learned and how my management philosophy evolved. One of the things you learn at Harvard Business School is that there is no one correct answer, no "school solution" in business. There are lots of ways to "skin the cat," to quote an old saying. Moreover, it is impossible to reduce contrarian thinking to a set of rules or a list of "dos and don'ts." By definition the contrarian reacts against set rules that become inviolate. For these reasons, a review of these two case histories—DLJ and Equitable—are really the best way for me to illustrate how contrarian thinking can be useful.

The first case will be Donaldson, Lufkin & Jenrette, Inc.—its early years, its midlife crisis, and its more recent renaissance, once again as a publicly owned company following a late-1995 offering of new stock and a partial sale by Equitable. The second case will be the Equitable experience, which began for me in 1985 when we sold DLJ to The

Equitable. Normally, one retires after selling one's company but I stuck around to help in the transition. One thing led to another and I was invited to become chairman, largely a ceremonial job at Equitable, in 1988. As storm clouds moved in, the board asked me to become president and chief executive officer as well in May 1990. My learning experience at Equitable escalated rapidly from that moment on.

In the closing chapters of this book, I offer some personal disciplines and suggestions, easily implemented by anyone, that have helped me in good times and especially in rough times. A few of these techniques might be classified as unconventional, controversial, or offbeat. They include the use of handwriting analysis, astrology, and personality tests—*anything* that helps me to understand people better. While I don't believe in poking into private lives unless work is being adversely affected, my lifelong fascination with what makes people tick, or "Sammy run," to use a few clichés from the past, has been my chief strength as a manager. Understanding people, how we are each different, is essential to being a successful manager. Most important of all, you have to understand yourself—your strengths and weaknesses as well as your aspirations in life.

THE DLJ
EXPERIENCE

Donaldson, Lufkin & Jenrette was the first securities firm started *de novo* in the post-World War II period. It was also the only new firm that became one of the top half dozen or so investment banks with revenues approaching $3.5 billion and pretax profits of $474 million in 1996. DLJ's infant money management organization blossomed into Alliance Capital Management, with $183 billion in assets under management, fee revenues approaching a $1 billion annual rate, and operating profits of just under $200 million. The two together have a market value in excess of $6 billion.

I wish I could say that the three founders had a clear vision from the start of what the firm could become one day. Our thinking never extended that far, nor would we have envisioned such success even in our wildest dreams. But what is amazing to me is the extent to which our original goals and objectives and the contrarian business strategy that we devised have continued to serve the firm so well through the years.

But there were many bumps along the way, as you will see.

THREE

THREE BRAINS
ARE BETTER
THAN ONE

When Bill Donaldson, Dan Lufkin, and I started DLJ in
1960, the first thing we learned is that three brains are
better than one. I was age 30 at the time, the "old man" of the
group. Donaldson and Lufkin, who had been classmates at
Yale, were a couple of years younger. The three of us had been
friends at the Harvard Business School. Our decision to form
Donaldson, Lufkin & Jenrette, Inc., was made after less than
three years working at different places on Wall Street. We
started the new firm with only $100,000 equity capital.

Our timing was propitious. It was one of those moments
when "youth will be served," with John F. Kennedy elected in
1960 as the nation's youngest President. People were starting
to dare to do things differently, and the stock market cooperat-
ed—always the *sine qua non* to a successful start-up on Wall
Street. Investors were beginning to look off the beaten path
for emerging growth companies—DLJ's stock-in-trade. Yet
despite these optimal conditions, I don't believe the firm
would have gone very far, given our limited experience, without three brains and differing points of view. Together we concocted something that was totally contrarian. As a result, DLJ
had no competition in the market we were serving in our early
years.

Dan Lufkin, a true contrarian, had the seminal idea for the
new firm's principal product—the then-unmet need for in-
depth research on small growth companies. Dan's thinking

had been greatly influenced by the writings of Phil Fisher, T. Rowe Price, and Thomas Brittingham, pioneers in investing in small growth companies. From his vantage point at Jeremiah Milbank's private investment office, Dan had observed that Wall Street research, to the extent it existed, was concentrated almost entirely on the large, old-line blue-chip stocks (like General Motors and U.S. Steel, two of the then current favorites of conservative investors).

Research reports, prepared by the "statistical departments" at firms like Merrill Lynch, were typically superficial, at the most one or two pages in length and aimed at individual or retail investors, the primary market until that time. Dan's vision for our product was in-depth research: 30- to 40-page reports, similar to the cases we had studied at Harvard Business School, on emerging growth companies. He believed that these young companies could run circles around the big lumbering, overpriced blue-chip stocks with their heavy over-head and bureaucratic procedures. Because of the lack of liquidity and investor unfamiliarity, Dan felt these long detailed analyses of all aspects of the company's operations were essential to assuring fiduciaries that there was real substance in these companies. In many ways, Dan Lufkin could be said to be the father of institutional research on Wall Street. DLJ literally took the green eye shades off the statisticians and recast them as glamorous, high-paid superstar analysts, replacing the "martini-drinking salesman" who previously had been regarded as the key to success in the institutional market. This ability to spot a new need, or a market not being served well, has been the key to DLJ's success over the years.

Interestingly, things have come full circle and much of Wall Street research today is again back to two to three pages. The content seems to me to be rather superficial and excessively short-term. So much more of the communication today is verbal, rather than the written word. I am told people no longer will read long research reports. In a market that always seems to go up, why bother? Yet the growing popularity of the Internet suggests that people still like to read in-depth information.

Bill Donaldson, usually more cautious compared to Dan Lufkin, was at his best in conceptualizing and articulating what the neophyte firm proposed to do—what President George Bush not so artfully called the "vision thing." Donaldson, incidentally, had many ties to George Bush and his family. Both he and Lufkin were Skull & Bones at Yale, although several classes after Bush. Donaldson roomed with George Bush's younger brother Jonathan. Too bad President Bush didn't have Donaldson by his side in articulating a vision for reelection. Donaldson also had worked on Wall Street for George Herbert Walker, namesake uncle to President Bush, prior to Bill's joining us in forming DLJ.

Bill Donaldson was early in detecting the ascendancy of institutional investors vis-à-vis the then-dominant retail or small individual investor market, so dear to the leadership of the New York Stock Exchange at the time under its leader Keith Funstan. Fidelity and Putnam were formed about this same time, as mutual funds began to gain in popularity, and money was pouring into corporate pension funds, with an increasing percentage earmarked for stocks. At the time we started DLJ, individual investors still accounted for 70 percent of all trading on the NYSE. This was, I suppose, ample justification for the Exchange's almost total preoccupation with small individual investors, but it was definitely not the way of the future. A decade later the percentages were reversed, with institutions accounting for 70 percent of trading volume. DLJ was in the forefront of this sea change. Once again contrarian thinking led us into an unexploited area—the newly emerging institutional investor market—where we had little or no competition at the outset because most of the major securities firms were still concentrating on serving individual investors.

Donaldson was also critical of the "club aspects" of the NYSE. At that time, all member firms had to be privately owned under NYSE rules. Each new partner or shareholder had to be approved by the Board of Governors of the Exchange. Effectively that meant there could be no publicly traded market in shares of member firms. While we were raising the initial capital for our new firm (from 10 friends and classmates), Donaldson frequently cited his belief that one day NYSE member firms would be publicly owned. It seemed absurd to Bill that member firms were urging the benefits of public ownership to corporate America while keeping their own doors barred to public ownership. While seemingly obvious today, at the time this was a totally contrarian view. Stock brokers going public—absurd! Here again Bill was prescient. A decade later, in 1970, DLJ became the first NYSE member firm to sell shares to the public, breaking down a 140-year barrier that had kept the NYSE privately owned and closed to public ownership. Others, including Merrill Lynch, soon followed.

Despite his criticism of the NYSE, Donaldson was the strongest believer, among the three of us, that our new firm should buy a seat on the Exchange (despite its high cost) and become a full-fledged member firm. Conceivably, we could have operated without an Exchange membership since most of the companies we expected to be recommending were not even listed on the NYSE. We could have bought their shares in the unlisted, over-the-counter market. But Donaldson was adamant that we needed what he called the "NYSE Good Housekeeping Seal of Approval," which its imprimatur would imply. He was right. We would have been ignored as a small over-the-counter dealer.

Ironically, Bill Donaldson, who was then so scornful of the NYSE's fixation on retail investors and its clublike environment, would himself become chairman and CEO of the Big Board some 20 years after leading the bitter fight to break down the barriers to public ownership of member firms. In that role, Bill once again demonstrated his vision, this time opening the eyes of the New York Stock Exchange to the need for more foreign listings, and longer trading hours, if New York and the NYSE were to maintain their dominance worldwide. As I recall, the Exchange establishment didn't particularly like that bit of advice either, but it was correct. I'd say Bill is batting three for three: he foresaw the coming dominance of institutional investors, the need for public ownership and more permanent capital for member firms, and more recently the need for the Exchange to become more global in outlook in serving foreign listings. Clearly Bill was good at the "vision thing." He was also contrarian in his thinking—all of these views were controversial and unconventional at the time.

My role in starting DLJ was far less visionary. Drawing on my experience at Brown Brothers Harriman & Company, which I had joined after Harvard Business School, I did get our new firm started in the asset management business, which I've always contended was, and still is, the best business on Wall Street. DLJ's fledgling money management business later grew into what is now Alliance Capital, with $183 billion assets under management at year-end 1996. My initial responsibilities also included setting up DLJ's back office, or securities clearing operations. In short, I was "Mr. Inside."

I also served as editor and a critic of all our research reports and other publications, sometimes reining in the "youthful enthusiasm" of my partners, both two years younger than my 30 years. The disciplines learned at a conservative old-line firm like Brown Brothers were helpful in tempering excessive exuberance. I tried to make our research reports balanced, with the risks as well as the opportunities disclosed. Dan and Bill took to calling me "Bear" because at that time of my life I seemed always to be focusing more on what could go wrong (somebody has to!). Indeed before we started the firm I recall attempting a little essay in Cartesian logic that showed that Lufkin's idea of preparing long research reports on small growth companies was totally uneconomic. I estimated the number of these long, detailed research studies that the three of us could be expected to produce in a year, multiplied that by a percentage of these companies' float (shares outstanding) that we could prudently buy for clients, and multiplied that by the commission per share (fixed by the New York Stock Exchange in those days) that we could earn. This rather simplistic analysis "proved" that the whole idea was uneconomic and that we could not expect to make a living out of commissions derived by buying and selling shares of a few small growth stocks.

What I had overlooked was that institutions would be so pleased with DLJ's unique in-depth research on small companies that they would reward us with other orders to buy and sell the big blue-chip stocks, even though we had not recommended them. Here Bill Donaldson's insistence that we join the NYSE was a godsend. Without a seat, we would have missed out on the most lucrative orders from institutional investors. With high fixed commission rates still in force on the NYSE (the commission per share was the same for a one-million-share order as for one hundred shares), we soon had a gusher of orders from big institutions who had excess commissions to give out and wanted to make sure that they were privy to DLJ's latest hot new recommendation. They also wanted to encourage better, in-depth research than what they were receiving from other investment companies. I don't think any of us at DLJ fully realized the extent of the huge and growing pot of fixed-rate commissions being generated by institutional investors, for which they at least *felt* they received very little in return. They were delighted to direct some of this largesse to DLJ in exchange for our in-depth research on small growth companies.

Because we literally invented in-depth research on small growth companies, we had no competition for several years, until others finally found out how profitable the business was—a classic example of the benefits of a contrarian strategy. By the time DLJ had imitators, we were well enough established to stand some competition. And the market kept growing and growing as more money flowed into institutional hands, and the institutions became increasingly active in managing their portfolios.

One of the firms that sought to replicate DLJ's early success in the institutional investor market was Carter, Berlin, Weill & Levitt (also Cogan along the way). The name has been changed many times since then, but its then-partners included Sandy Weill, now spectacularly successful as chief executive officer of The Travelers Group, and Arthur Levitt, the most knowledgeable chairman of the Securities and Exchange Commission in my experience. They were an interesting group, though we viewed them initially as imitators of the DLJ format.

Interestingly, Sandy Weill never really became successful in a big way until he became a contrarian and stopped trying to replicate DLJ (which he did with some success in the late 1960s). By successfully identifying the retail investor market as a reemerging area of opportunity during the disarray of the 1970s (about 20 years ahead of Morgan Stanley's recent discovery of retail investors at Dean Witter), Sandy became a true contrarian, when everyone else (except Merrill Lynch) had turned their back on individual investors. More recently, his success has become legendary with his highly successful forays into insurance at a time when others were exiting the field. Sandy knows how to turn a problem into an opportunity, the hallmark of a contrarian manager.

The fact that I did *not* follow my Cartesian logic that suggested that DLJ's initial business strategy was uneconomic and instead elected to cast my lot with Bill Donaldson and Dan Lufkin in this new venture is evidence that I was and am a card-carrying contrarian. Even though I thought our business plan was full of flaws, I put this aside because I had observed, first at Harvard Business School and then in New York City, that Bill Donaldson and Dan Lufkin were winners. They were two of the most dynamic, bright, attractive, articulate, and well-connected people that I had ever met. They seemed to know everyone. I knew that, one way or another, they would succeed, and I wanted to be part of that success. I also had observed that at Brown Brothers Harriman & Company, where I worked, almost *all* the partners were Yale graduates (not boding too well for this University of North Carolina graduate!) and that it seemed to take about 20 years to "make partner." So my choice wasn't so hard to make. In the end, I concluded we could always make some money investing for the firm's account even if the stock brokerage business did not prove lucrative. Interestingly, in later years after fixed commission rates were ended, this has become a key source of profits through DLJ's red-hot merchant banking group.

Incidentally, lest the above appears to reflect unkindly on Brown Brothers Harriman & Company, it is *not* so intended. Brown Brothers was a great experience for me. It taught me how to do things first-class and made an indelible imprint on my psyche. In many ways it was like an elegant finishing school (though this remark probably won't make my friends there very happy either). The high ethical standards, the client orientation, and the general classiness of the firm made it a model for me. DLJ today even looks like Brown Brothers Harriman on the inside, replete with ancestral prints of early Wall Street leaders, including John Trumbull's great portrait of Alexander Hamilton and a Gilbert Stuart of George Washington. We have out-Brown-Brothered Brown Brothers. I felt the new firm needed the cachet of antiquity, something only a contrarian would try to impose on a brand-new firm. To those who might think this an example of corporate excess, I would only note that all these artifacts have appreciated spectacularly in value over the years. We bought them when nobody wanted them—but like Warren Buffett, we aren't selling. They become rarer and more valuable every year.

The fact is Brown Brothers Harriman & Company has been in business since 1818, and has remained very profitable. The firm must be full of contrarians, having resisted so many of the trends—including remaining a private partnership while all other banks went public. It's a firm worth studying and evaluating from a management point of view. They are clearly doing something right. Perhaps their secret *is* secrecy. The firm has always been very private and circumspect about divulging its sources of profitability.

TRY TO HIRE SOMEBODY SMARTER THAN YOU ARE

DLJ's initial success was such that we were soon back at Harvard Business School seeking new recruits. While a successful idea has many authors, I probably was most responsible for an early DLJ guiding principle that still to this day is quoted around the firm: "Try to hire someone smarter than you are," to which we quickly affixed, "and they will make *you* look good." In the previous chapter I noted that my go–no-go decision to join DLJ was based almost entirely on my view that Bill Donaldson and Dan Lufkin were two smart cookies; I knew they would succeed. That decision was right, and I was determined that in the future DLJ would hire only "the best and the brightest" as we sought to create a sort of Camelot on Wall Street (Camelot, by the way, was very much "in" during the 1960s, not only as a Broadway musical but as a description of the young Kennedy Administration, which saw itself as a modern-day King Arthur's court).

The simple idea that you should try to hire someone smarter than yourself was probably my best contribution to the evolution of DLJ in its formative years. I coordinated recruiting from the start and installed myself as a sort of fraternity rushing chairman, utilizing a very valuable management experience from my college fraternity days at Chapel Hill. A college fraternity membership is totally changed every four years. If you have a couple of bad years' "rushes" in a row, the place starts to wither away. Three strikes, you're dead. Companies have a longer cycle, and failure to recruit well in a given year can usually be made up later. But the principle is largely the same. Companies have to keep recruiting and bringing in bright people or they atrophy and become insular and out of touch. This is a somewhat contrarian view in an era when cost cutting is the great management god in American business. While cost cutting is important and may be imperative in some situations, such as I found at Equitable, I have always held the view that no company ever became great by cost cutting. At some point you've got to get back on a growth cycle. Otherwise, it's a race to the bottom with one round of cost cutting followed by another until one day there's nothing left.

The lesson I learned at DLJ is that you have to keep bringing in bright people if you want to keep growing. While I don't want to denigrate the importance of cost cutting under some circumstances—I certainly did my share at Equitable—I worry that some companies are cutting loose valued employees that they will need fairly soon. If we examine the demographics of the work force, the supply of new young people coming into the labor force is starting to slack off. The current "Generation X," which has had trouble finding employment in a corporate downsizing environment, will be strictly in demand before their cycle has run its course.

Starting with our very first year, upstart DLJ began to recruit at Harvard Business School side by side with all the great American corporations and financial institutions. Talk about chutzpah! We soon expanded our recruiting to Stanford, Wharton, and other leading business schools as our needs grew. Even though we were only looking for a few recruits in those early years, the mystique of the firm and the students' interest in entrepreneurial job opportunities was such that, almost embarrassingly, we usually had far more Harvard MBAs lining up to interview at DLJ than was the case for Chase Bank, Ford Motor, Merrill Lynch, or Morgan Stanley (which at that time was still somnolent, living off its Morgan past, and had not blossomed into the competitive force that it is today). DLJ was really the *only* small firm recruiting seriously at the business schools at that time—once again, a contrarian manager's dream situation which gave us a fast start in the race for the best brains.

Since our aim was to hire people brighter than we were, we put great emphasis on academic standing in our selection process. Donaldson and Lufkin also used to ask, "Would you like to have dinner with this person?" While other achievements and the overall impression made in the interview were important, the sine qua non for me was academic achievement, no matter how personable the job candidate. In the end, it seemed you had to be bright *and* a good dinner companion to get a job at DLJ. Of the first dozen MBAs we hired, 10 were either Baker Scholars at Harvard Business School (top 3 percent of class) or Phi Beta Kappa in their undergraduate years. From then on it became a snowball effect. The word got out that DLJ was the hot place for the best and brightest people to go. We were overwhelmed with job applications from bright MBAs. I should put in a disclaimer here: I've learned over the years that you don't have to be a Baker Scholar or a Phi Beta Kappa or even a college graduate to succeed on Wall Street or anywhere else—as long as you are very bright! The problem is how to find these bright people.

Early on we elected to confine our recruiting to graduate business schools. Their graduates had been prescreened and were already committed to a business career. Moreover, this avoided the necessity of our having to set up an elaborate and expensive management development program, as was the case at the banks who tended to recruit directly from undergraduate schools. It always seemed to me far more cost-efficient to recruit from the graduate business schools.

Although we could hire only a very few of the hundreds of young MBAs who signed up each year to interview with DLJ, our extensive recruiting at business schools also served an important ancillary role as a showcase for the new firm to an influential future market. We made every effort to turn people down gracefully to avoid hurt feelings. In later years, many of those we interviewed and did not hire still became valued

clients or good friends of the firm. All these interviews at top
business schools helped enormously in building awareness
and understanding of the new firm and its management
philosophies.

Another management principle related to hiring that we
evolved was a belief that to grow you have to continually add
bright people. This was based on a view that a bright person
creates his own market (we may have gotten this idea from
Peter Drucker, who consulted with us in our early years). I
actually charted this out a half dozen years after the firm started; I found that DLJ's top-line revenue growth directly corre-
lated with the growth in size of our professional staff. The one
year we slowed down our recruiting for cost-control reasons
was followed by a slowdown in revenue growth the following
year. Since we were not paying these young MBAs anything
like the incremental revenue growth they generated, there was
an obvious beneficial effect on DLJ's bottom-line profitability.
We may have been the first Wall Street firm to discover just
how profitable it was to hire bright young MBAs. Goldman
Sachs and Morgan Stanley soon caught on, and up went the
price tag for freshly minted MBAs.

Under this theory, you could not hire too many bright people. While we believed this generally to be true, the practical
application had to be tempered by our ability to assimilate new
recruits each year. Our on-the-job training consisted of assign-
ing each new recruit to DLJ's investment research department,
the core of our activities at the time. Everyone was expected to
be an analyst first, before moving into other areas of the firm.
While this is no longer the case in today's more specialized
world, everyone is still expected to think like an analyst. DLJ
still calls itself "the house that research built," the tag line on
a home-grown ad I concocted for DLJ years ago.

Let me conclude this chapter with a couple of thoughts on
recruiting. First, I strongly believe most senior managements
of most U.S. companies don't pay enough attention to recruiting and assimilating new recruits into their organizations.
They are the lifeblood of a successful growth company. For at
least the first 25 years of DLJ's existence, I coordinated and

led the recruiting personally, spending at least a couple of days each year on campus interviewing students. John Chalsty has continued this tradition as DLJ's current CEO. Forty years after graduating, he was back at the Harvard Business School recruiting for DLJ earlier this year. This may sound like overkill for a CEO, but I always learned a lot about what students were thinking, how they viewed DLJ, and what our competitors were doing and saying. It was also fun. For me those interviews were like going back to the fountain of youth at Academia. I also accepted speaking engagements at the top business schools whenever possible. Communicating with bright young people helps you stay young in attitude and outlook. They will get you out of your ivory tower very quickly!

Second, I would like to point out that my admonition to "hire someone brighter than yourself" is diametrically opposed (and therefore contrarian) to the more prevalent management attitude in most companies. Tony O'Reilly, the colorful CEO of H. J. Heinz Company, relates the advice he received from an old-time mentor when he first became CEO of H. J. Heinz. "The first and most important thing for a new CEO to do is to identify his successor—and then fire the S.O.B.!" Bright newcomers all too often are seen as competition for the top spot in what is perceived as a zero-sum game, at least managerially. The worst managers, of course, surround themselves with seemingly nonthreatening sycophants who will never be candidates to succeed their boss. Nothing could be more dangerous to a company's existence than the presence of a virus that discourages or kills off bright newcomers.

Finally—and this may sound like the truism of all time—managing a company is so easy if you hire bright people. They don't need to be told what to do, they already have built-in inner drives and personal incentives to excel. Just point them in the direction you want to go. As a result of DLJ's recruiting at top business schools over the past 35 years, I never have had to worry about management succession. There are layers and layers of bright people who have the capability of running the place. And I must say that John Chalsty, DLJ's current CEO, whom I recruited many years ago, is Exhibit A of the principle "Hire someone smarter than yourself and they will make you look good." John has made *me* (as well as himself) look very good in leading DLJ to new heights.

I have said nothing here about hiring experienced people away from other firms, since in our early years, when DLJ was narrowly focused, we almost entirely grew our professional staff by recruiting young MBAs. But having everyone come up the same route can also create a certain insularity and smugness. As DLJ later expanded into other areas, such as investment banking and fixed income, most of our early hires came from the competition. A good example is DLJ's current president and COO, Joe Roby. While Joe had the (then) almost obligatory Harvard MBA, he cut his teeth in Kidder Peabody's investment banking group. Under the legendary Al Gordon, Kidder was known for its aggressiveness in soliciting new investment banking clients. Joe brought that competitiveness with him to DLJ at a time when the firm had gotten a bit smug. New blood always helps.

I should also tell you about the one who got away—Mike Milken. Long before Milken became king of junk bonds, he was a well-respected research-oriented bond manager at Drexel, very unhappy with the changes in that company's ownership. I popped down to Philadelphia, took him to dinner, and subsequently offered him a job with DLJ in New York as head of our new fixed-income group. Mike replied that he liked and respected DLJ but wanted to return to his native Los Angeles. If DLJ would open an office there, he would join us. At the time, all of us at DLJ felt strongly that our activities should be centralized in New York City (a view long since discarded). So we parted company. I've always wondered what Mike Milken's career would have been like had he joined us and come to New York. Twenty years later, after Drexel's demise, DLJ has become number one in the high-yield bond area that Mike pioneered.

THE CARE AND FEEDING OF CREATIVE PEOPLE

Despite DLJ's good success in recruiting bright people out of the business schools, we soon were confronted with a different set of problems. How do you retain and motivate these bright people once they become less starry-eyed and their talents are more visible to the world and one's competitors? Early on, the care and feeding of bright people became another challenge to our contrarian management style.

The bright, creative, entrepreneurial types we sought to hire and blend into our organization dictated a rather different form of organization. For starters, it had to be more horizontal in nature than the traditional vertical, chain-of-command organization that characterizes most companies (in the military-styled command-and-control form of organization). I have always disliked these hierarchical structures. They tend to stifle creativity on the front lines since all wisdom is perceived to flow from above. The presence of a visible pyramidal hierarchy also tends to breed a sort of zero-sum game mentality. There is only one chief executive officer, one chief operating officer, one chief financial officer, etc. To succeed, you have to attain one of these jobs. Competition for these limited posts creates a dog-eat-dog sort of environment that is anathema to creative types who disdain to play office politics, leapfrogging over or cannibalizing their colleagues. To counter this mentality, we always spoke of the virtues of rapid growth and a greatly expanding pie. With continued growth the financial and career opportunities for existing members of the firm would be enhanced, not diluted, by talented new entrants. We never thought we were in a zero-sum game or that there were limits to our ability to grow. And so there were no limits to bringing in new entrepreneurial people, who had the potential to create their own market.

Our challenge was to create a collegial environment where the presence of so many bright people was an intellectual turn-on, so to speak, rather than a disincentive. I believe DLJ has been extremely successful for the most part in creating such an environment, witness the very low turnover of key personnel over the years and the continued ability to attract bright people. Indeed, it is remarkable how many of those who left later returned, better able to appreciate the environment we had created at DLJ. Most who left usually felt good about their DLJ experience and many became valued clients of the firm.

What were the key elements that led to this success in retaining and motivating bright people?

First we had to establish an environment of professionalism. Our corporate goals and objectives, nonexistent or ignored in so many companies, were genuinely helpful in establishing the tone of professionalism that we sought. These objectives were essentially contrarian in nature, replete with high-sounding admonitions to:

- Provide high-value-added services that meet the changing needs of our clients, rather than repeat what others are already doing well (certainly the essence of a contrarian business philosophy—do it differently).
- Be a leader in all the activities that we undertake.
- Concentrate on high-end institutional and corporate markets, where the demand for excellence and the rewards are commensurate with the creative resources of our professional staff (at the time others were ignoring the institutional investor market).
- Avoid low-margin repetitive businesses, where the rewards are the product of the ever-more-efficient processing of transactions. (We disdained so-called commodity businesses

where our services could not be differentiated from the competition and therefore more prone to price competition.)

- Achieve a level of profitability commensurate with the human resources of the firm as well as the capital resources employed. Translated, this meant that we had to be profitable enough to pay the competitive compensation levels needed to attract and hold our professional staff while still earning a superior return on our capital.

- Create a highly professional organization that demands excellence from itself. This meant we were our own most severe critics.

- Maintain the highest standards of integrity. We always regarded this as the single most important objective—the one thing that could never be compromised.

- Have fun—the famous final corporate objective of DLJ. *Having fun* was defined as the satisfaction of doing an excellent job for clients, the satisfaction of a job well done, as opposed to uproarious office parties (there were a few of those also). If you are going to spend such long hours at work, it should be fun.

Another unstated goal was not to take ourselves too seriously, to have balance in our lives. This was and remains a truly contrarian view that not only differentiates DLJ but helps avoid early burnout, a common Wall Street disease, which most of us at DLJ escaped.

We most certainly overworked the word *professionalism* in the early years, but even today at DLJ we refer to the firm's "professional staff." This was not just an elite cadre but included virtually everyone, down to the janitor. We wanted everyone to think and act as a professional. The word *employee* was not in our lexicon—we called them "associates." We did not want people to think or act like employees. The term employee had a distinctly distasteful ring in our ears. Some things do change with time, though. When I returned to DLJ recently I was given an employee identification card. Security reasons were cited, but I wish we could have called it something else.

Another credo that we developed very early was that *true* professionals want to be surrounded by other professionals— not *hacks,* a term of derision at DLJ whose origin probably traces to my college journalism career. (Hack writers were unprofessional and held in low repute by their more professional colleagues.) The key, of course, was to *maintain uniform excellence* throughout the professional staff. This created pride and was self-reenforcing. I suppose it's a bit like one rotten apple spoiling the barrel. We were always on the alert to weed out individuals who did not meet our standards of professionalism and excellence. The result was a superior esprit de corps in which members were proud to be a part of an elite fraternity. This still seems to be the case at DLJ even though the corps has grown to nearly 6,000 individuals.

Another key element in DLJ's ability to attract, hold, and motivate bright people was our early decision to concentrate on what we called high-end or high-value-added markets. Translated more literally, this meant that the firm had decided to concentrate on institutional and corporate markets, where the demands for excellence were very high and the payoff commensurate with the skills required. Of course, we also happened to think that the institutional market was where the growth would be. In many ways, the story of DLJ is a 35-year play on the institutionalization of the capital markets, which is still continuing as money pours into mutual funds. We studiously, even religiously, avoided the type of mass-market, retail business which would have involved selling our services to small individual investors.

It was not a case of our being snobs, but rather our view that the mass-market culture was not the most conducive environment to creativity. We felt this business was too time consuming and had a limited payoff, which in turn would have meant hiring lesser mortals to service that business. Over the years I have observed that it is very hard to mix the two cultures—one tends to drive out the other. Now we are about to witness the coming together of the ultimate high-end firm—Morgan Stanley—with Dean Witter, Discover, a mass-market retailer. My only advice to the happy couple would be to try to keep the two cultures separate. In the securities industry, Merrill Lynch has come closest to achieving a blending of mass-market brawn and brains. Believe me, there were many times when I tired of coping with the prima donna, super star mentality that sometimes goes with the high-end, high-value-added business. I have admired and envied the marketing muscle commanded by a succession of capable Merrill Lynch CEO's, such as Don Regan, Bill Schreyer, and Dan Tully, Merrill's current CEO. You want these guys by your side when the going gets tough. Dick Fisher and John Mack at Morgan Stanley must have reached the same conclusion.

Over the years it seems that the mass-market firms like Merrill are constantly trying to trade up, while the high-end firms like Morgan Stanley, Goldman Sachs, and DLJ occasionally find themselves redefining some previously avoided markets as now being high-end (such as high-net-worth individuals) in an effort to broaden their distribution. Now Morgan Stanley has decided to leap in up to its neck in the belief that individual investors now hold the key to the future. Time will tell. I still think they are two totally different businesses.

At DLJ, we rather early resolved this need for some mass-market exposure by a contrarian solution. Instead of hiring a lot of retail salespeople, thereby playing catch-up with Merrill Lynch and other big retail houses, we leapfrogged by acquiring Pershing & Company, a highly regarded New York correspondent firm serving a network of regional brokerage firms, whose clients for the most part were small individual investors. Pershing's clients at the time included the most prestigious regional securities firms, giving us correspondent relationships throughout the nation. Pershing, now a division of DLJ, executes and clears more than 10 percent of all securities transactions on the New York Stock Exchange for some 600 small- and medium-size securities firms, which lack the scale to have their own back office (a term we studiously avoided at DLJ as being demeaning to those who performed the vital custodian transactions, clearing, and service functions). Gene Messenkopf, a CPA who started what would have been called DLJ's back office, advised us over and over never to use that term. Gene was seeking the same professionalism and high standards of excellence in his area that we sought to inculcate among our investment bankers, analysts, and portfolio managers.

In any event, the addition of Pershing gave DLJ access to an efficient, low-cost processing capacity for its own trades as well as indirect participation in the mass market of retail investors served by our correspondents. As a result, we were able to focus DLJ's professional staff on the needs of the institutional and corporate markets while still enjoying indirect participation in the retail markets through Pershing. In acquiring Pershing, we did violate one of our rules to avoid low-margin processing, repetitive businesses. But Pershing met the even more important DLJ guideline of being a leader in all we undertook. Pershing was the clear number one in correspondent clearing and has gone on to even greater success and profitability under DLJ's banner. Though the margins were low, the return on equity has been high.

All these moves helped maintain an environment of professionalism at DLJ, which was very helpful in keeping our brain trust happy—but what about compensation? I quickly learned that creative people are, if anything, even more focused on their compensation than seems to be the case with less entrepreneurial types. As a result, we always asked our professionals to prepare written self-evaluations of their major accomplishments during the year together with their goals and objectives for the coming year (which would be used in the subsequent year's evaluation). This assured that no good deed would go unnoticed as we came up with annual bonus recommendations. Here are some of the guidelines we used in determining incentive compensation:

First, as chief executive officer never hesitate to pay others more than you are making yourself. I cannot recall a time at DLJ when, in a given year, I was the highest-paid executive. This is the single best antidote to the dangerous virus that says everyone has to aspire to be CEO of the company in order to be successful. In a given year, there should be many professionals on the staff who are more highly compensated than the CEO.

Second, compensation should be directly related to performance; in other words, it should be true incentive compensation. Compensation at DLJ was always a combination of individual performance, business unit performance, and overall firm performance. There were some lean years, however, when we elected to sacrifice firm performance to keep our core professional staff together. In theory, it should be symmetrical, when firm profits go up, bonuses go up and vice versa. But Wall Street is notable for the ease of mobility from one firm to the next. All you have to do is go across the street to get a new job. You don't have to relocate your house or your kids' school. Warren Buffett learned this the hard way when he sought to impose the logic of symmetrical compensation when Salomon had a bad year. The result was a major loss of talent to competitors in Wall Street's favorite game of musical chairs.

I can recall one Christmas bonus time when we were barely at breakeven and I felt like Old Mother Hubbard whose cupboard was so bare. How to avoid a brain drain to Goldman Sachs and Morgan Stanley? Because of the professional working environment we had created at DLJ, no one *wanted* to leave. But they needed reassurance that the firm not only would survive the financial crisis but had a bright future. People also want to know that they are needed, and I let them know in one-on-one meetings how much I was counting on each of them. In such times, the legacy of love and care you have invested in these bright people in the past is crucial. You can't just suddenly become caring and expect to be believed. The lesson I learned is that you can't just rely on money to keep people—sometimes you'll find you don't have any—but if you have been sensitive and have articulated a vision of the future, most of them will stick with you. Money isn't everything, even on Wall Street.

While I was willing to go all the way down to breakeven to keep our people from leaving, I drew the line there. After a humiliating operating loss in 1974, my first year as DLJ's CEO, I took a vow (like Scarlett O'Hara in *Gone With the Wind*): "As God is my witness, I'll never lose money again." (I think she said, "I'll never go hungry again.") DLJ never has lost money since then, and later went on to 28 consecutive quarters of earnings up over the prior year's same quarter. (I had to take the vow all over again after Equitable's big loss in 1991.)

Third, compensation should be skewed heavily toward the year-end bonus rather than base salary. In the volatile securities industry, it is vital to keep fixed costs (and breakeven) low. At DLJ, for example, base salaries were only about a third of those that I encountered at Equitable (although the aggregate, including bonus, was much higher). Granted DLJ is in a more cyclical business than a life insurance company, there is no doubt that this disparity drives the DLJ people to achieve maximum profitability. Incidentally, I have never believed in the value of small annual increases in base salary, which can be perceived as an entitlement. I read something once about a just noticeable difference, or JND, principle in giving raises. The author held that very small (1 to 2 percent) annual salary increases were not noticeable to the recipient and, therefore, were a waste of corporate money. Far better to wait for a raise until the amount would be noticeable (5 to 6 percent or more). The JND was said to vary from business to business; you have to define what it is for your business. Generally, with regard to executive compensation, our practice at DLJ was to give base salary increases only on rare occasions—a new job, a new title, etc.—rather than the creeping inflation of annual entitlements of small raises. Varying the bonus each year is a far better way to reward good and bad performance. Keep the base salary low.

As to the size of the bonus, I have always felt strongly that there should be no ceiling or caps, either on the size of the overall bonus pool or payments to individuals. This runs counter to the recommendation of many consultants for set "target bonuses" if certain goals are met, which are then capped no matter how high the profitability. Guess what? Profits never rise above the level to meet the target bonus. The managers find some way to defer them to the following year. For this reason, I prefer a straight percentage of profits, as opposed to bonuses based on achieving plan or capped at some level. Let's go onward and upward should be the marching order.

Interestingly, I have always been surprised how important *relative* compensation is in the eyes of creative, entrepreneurial types (maybe to everybody!). On many occasions, I have seen executives thrilled to learn the absolute size of their bonus turn sour later when the office grapevine or public documents disclose relative compensation among key executives.

While this may sound like the softest touch of all time, I have always found it useful to ask key executives what they feel is a fair bonus for their performance. Over and over, I have found they usually come up with lower figures than what I had in mind. On the rare occasion when the executive proposed a higher bonus than what seemed fair to me, the resulting discussion was useful in clarifying the differences. Overall, the effect of this technique is to make the executives feel in control of their destiny and livelihood (*empowered* seems to be the modern term of choice)—a very happy feeling. Obviously, one can follow this intensive technique only with direct reports. I encouraged others to follow a similar process with their direct reports.

The use of equity (direct ownership or options) as an incentive device in my opinion is greatly overrated. We used direct equity ownership in DLJ's early years when we were still privately owned, inviting key players to buy in at net asset (book) value, supposedly a privilege. It was more symbolic of being "admitted to the club," which may have had greater incentive value than any actual rewards that were realized. After DLJ's IPO, we used options. The decade-long bear market, really from 1973 to 1982 (which seems inconceivable to today's entrepreneurs and younger investors) very quickly reduced the value people attached to their options.

The trouble with options is that they are dependent at least as much on the vagaries of the market as on the company's performance. They obviously have worked well over the past 15 years, when the stock market has compounded at a remarkable (but unsustainable) 15 percent annual rate. The market has been rather like the "tooth fairy" in rewarding executives instead of the companies having to pay big bonuses. Since a rising tide lifts all boats, even mediocre corporate and individual performance has been rewarded. While options have worked extremely well in recent years in enriching executives, excessive dependence on options is a double-edged sword when bad markets come along, as they inevitably do. Nothing is more demoralizing than to have a great business year but to have your compensation reduced or wiped out because the stock market had a bad year. That is when cash on the barrel-head comes back in style as compensation.

A CONTRARIAN BUSINESS STRATEGY FOR DLJ

We never started out to construct a contrarian business strategy when we formed Donaldson, Lufkin & Jenrette. Indeed, I don't recall that we even thought of ourselves as contrarians. Yale and Harvard Business School were about as mainstream establishment as one could get on Wall Street at the time. Rather it was the financial imperatives of our meager resources—a puny $100,000 equity (although that seemed a lot bigger in 1960!)—as well as our perception of where the opportunity lay.

We sincerely believed that small growth stocks represented the best investment opportunity vis-à-vis the old-line blue-chip stocks that had done so well in the 1950s post-World War II Eisenhower years. Bill Donaldson kept insisting that we needed what he called (with his superior Yale freshman French) a raison d'être for the firm, or something that we could hand out to clients or investors to explain why we were forming a new firm. So we finally sat down and tried to put all this in writing. The result was a small booklet entitled *Common Stock and Common Sense*. To my amazement it still is quoted today and has become something of a collectors' item. Indeed DLJ reprinted it some 20 years later, but the little booklets, which are in short supply, are still in demand by old-timers (and some newcomers) who prize them.

The first part of *Common Stock and Common Sense* was written by me, drawing on my Brown Brothers Harriman &

Company experience with blue-chip stocks. I noted that during the 1950s (the decade preceding the formation of DLJ)
the blue-chip stocks, as measured by the Dow Jones and
Standard & Poor's averages, had *tripled* in value. Yet during
the same decade there had been *zero* net growth in corporate
earnings (the latter Eisenhower years had been marked by
recession as the nation tried to lick what by today's standards
was an infinitesimal trade and budget deficit). What that
meant was that the entire tripling in market value reflected a
widening of price-earnings ratios, from some 7 times earnings
at the beginning of the decade to 20 to 21 times earnings at
the time of DLJ's founding (sounds like the past decade!). My
simple, no-brainer conclusion was that obviously this growing
discrepancy between earnings growth and market appreciation
could not go on indefinitely. For comparable future market
appreciation, one would have to "look off the beaten path" (a
term I copied from my mentor Bud Newquist at Brown
Brothers Harriman & Co., although BBH & Co. was scarcely
known for looking off the beaten path). In the Nirvana we saw
off the beaten path, investors could find not only more rapid
earnings growth in smaller companies but far lower price-
earnings ratios. Dan and Bill took it from there. Lufkin, in
particular, laid out his passionately held belief that small, well-
managed companies could run circles around the big bureaucratic multitiered so-called blue chips, which he proceeded to
consign to the dustbin.

Well, it worked, at least for a couple of years, when the
"baby blue chips" far outperformed the old-line favorites,
allowing us to get off to a fast start. Timing is everything in a
venture like ours with limited resources. Our raison d'être in
the form of *Common Stock and Common Sense* was widely
circulated in the investment community. The title, of course,
could apply to *all* common stocks, even though our *spécialité
du maison* was small growth stocks. The result of our little
booklet was to firmly establish DLJ as being on the side of
those favoring higher percentages of common stocks in institutional portfolios. Amazingly at that time, bonds comprised
70 percent or more of most pension funds and other institutional portfolios.

So we started out with a contrarian product—common stocks of small growth companies—as opposed to the blue-chip stocks *and* bonds that were so much in favor with institutional and individual investors in 1960, as the Kennedy years, which were also the early DLJ years, began.

Lacking a sales force, we also conveniently consigned the "martini-drinking salesman" (martinis were waning in popularity in the 1960s) to the dustbin. We felt that the new breed of institutional investor wanted to talk directly to the analyst who had done the research, rather than through a sales intermediary. And so we conceived the concept of the analyst-salesman. There was supposed to be sort of a virtuous circle effect—not only did the institutional portfolio manager benefit from talking directly to the analyst, but our own analysts would be sharper and better for the experience, emerging from the ivory tower (or statistical department) to which they were normally consigned at other firms.

All these neat concepts began to wither away in the prosperity that followed. The firm's business got so good and the demand on our analysts' time became so great that we found it necessary to bring back the salesman, not as a martini drinker but a much more professional type able to help the analyst navigate the increasingly complicated maze of portfolio managers, analysts, and traders that began to emerge at the large institutions. We also had to hire a large cadre of traders at DLJ to interface with their counterparts at institutions and manage risk as block trading and position bids became equally or more important than research in determining order flow from the large institutions. Goldman Sachs, under the legendary Gus Levy, pioneered block trading, in which a portion of the firm's capital was committed to facilitate large trades, which then meant buying tag ends of blocks of stock when buyers could not be immediately found. This is one case in which we found it necessary to be an imitator, but we, along with Bear Stearns, were probably only the second or third firms to make extensive use of firm capital to facilitate block trades in equities. Truman Bidwell, a highly regarded trader on the floor of the NYSE whom I had gotten to know through my college fraternity days, was instrumental in convincing us that DLJ would gain an important competitive edge if we would put some of our capital at risk to facilitate large block trades. He was right—our block trading business soared. The institutions much preferred to buy and sell in large blocks rather than "dribbling" shares out gradually over days and weeks. The private partnerships hated the risks they would have had to take in buying large blocks of stock into their own inventories even though the block might be resold quickly. There was always the risk the market would take a nose dive before the block could be resold. Years later when DLJ was making its case for more capital and public ownership for member firms, we cited the growing demand by institutional investors to trade in huge blocks, requiring some block positioning by the member firm.

Five years after the firm started—in 1965—we also cast aside the religion of investing only in small growth companies. John Corcoran, our chief investment strategist at the time, decreed to the world that "there is no longer a scarcity of growing earning power" (the Kennedy tax cut having rekindled growth in the economy during the 1960s). "Ergo," Corcoran intoned, "DLJ no longer believed it necessary only to look off the beaten path to find growing earning power." Moreover, many of these small growth companies now were selling at two to three times the price-earnings multiples of the lumbering old blue chips—just the reverse of the conditions prevailing when DLJ began in 1960. We shocked our small-growth-company cult by recommending—of all things—the purchase of General Motors. This was almost heresy to our growth clients at the time. O. J. Anderson, one of our top analysts, discovered or invented something called a *scrappage ratio* that suggested GM's automobile sales would grow again for an extended period. They did, for a while. Miraculously, GM stock nearly doubled over the next year or two, and DLJ's mystique was further burnished since we were perceived as flexible enough to adapt to changing times. It was a contrarian call at the time, since even the most conservative investors had come to disdain GM. I can't recall if anyone at DLJ ever said "sell General Motors"—I hope so. Even the scrappage ratio couldn't save the company from a combination of inept management, greedy unions, high oil prices, and the Japanese small car inroads, all of which combined to erode GM's dominance.

The popularity and wide acceptance of DLJ's in-depth research, which we expanded to include John Corcoran's "top down" macrostrategies, emboldened us to expand in other areas. Most successful was our decision to integrate backward into asset management, or money management, as the old investment counsel business had come to be known. Once again we were challenging the orthodoxy that only large, well-known bank trust departments could be trusted to manage corporate pension funds. We also had found another market that was not being well served. The banks had been too conservative, even arrogant, in their conviction that only a bank trust department was qualified to manage pension money.

Conceptually, instead of solely making *components* (our individual company research ideas) DLJ now would make complete *systems*. This was a fancy way of saying we would assume full management of the portfolio rather than picking just individual stocks. It also meant that we would be competing with our institutional customers. DLJ had always had a small money management operation from day one, which I literally ran out of my hip pocket while doing research and acting as the firm's chief administrative officer. That humble beginning—the discretionary management of funds for a few friends and classmates—took a quantum leap in 1963 when Dick Hexter, our technology analyst, convinced Litton Industries to turn $10 million over to DLJ to manage, using the firm's highly regarded research.

At the time, pension management was dominated by the banks, who had earlier wrested the business away from the insurance companies, who had dominated in the early post-World War II period. Typically, a single bank trust department managed a company's *entire* pension fund. Brash DLJ argued—sotto voce, of course—that the banks needed some competition (Bill Donaldson called it a "burr under the saddle") to stimulate better performance. In 1963, Litton Industries was perceived to be perhaps the most avant garde technology company in America, a real opinion leader in the business world, led by the cerebral Roy Ash. Whatever Litton did, others emulated and followed. And so we soon received similar-sized accounts from pension funds at General Foods, General Mills, and Whirlpool—all seeking to stimulate competition for their bank managers. Ford Motor came in soon thereafter. Some were linked to Litton through overlapping directorships. And we were suddenly on our way to being a major asset manager. The market was ripe for new competition.

It would not be an exaggeration to claim seminal credit (or blame?) on behalf of DLJ for the entire trend toward the use of multiple portfolio managers in managing U.S. corporate pension funds and for the concept of performance measurement that resulted from using competitive managers. Corporate concerns about fiduciary liabilities had gradually melted away as the stock market rose steadily. The banks, saddled by too many bonds, too little in stocks, and unwilling to pay the price of hiring the best portfolio management talent, began to slip in investment performance. Morgan Bank was a notable exception. DLJ's innovative idea of having multiple managers to create a spirit of competition spread like wildfire.

Hand in hand with the use of competitive multiple managers came a new development, performance measurement. Until the mid-1960s, very little attention had been paid to short-term, or even long-term, investment performances, since typically companies used only one bank or insurance company to manage their pension funds. The investment world hasn't been the same since performance measurement between competitive managers swept on the scene. "Active" portfolio management, involving far more portfolio turnover than was the case in the banks' heyday, became the order of the day as portfolio managers strove to improve their results. And with this increased trading activity, came more demands on Wall Street for capital to facilitate the new demand by their managers for instant liquidity.

DLJ's fledgling money management business grew into what is now called Alliance Capital Management, one of the world's largest asset managers, whose funds under management now (30 years later) exceed $180 billion. The name change, from DLJ to Alliance in the 1970s, helped diffuse conflict of interest concerns over having a broker-dealer money manager, raised when Congress passed the new Employee Retirement Income Security Act (ERISA) legislation in 1974. The name change also had the double benefit of slightly camouflaging the fact that DLJ was competing so successfully with its institutional investor clients, especially the banks. Alliance *sounded* like a different company—and it was—even though DLJ owned 100 percent of it until the sale to Equitable in 1985, when Alliance was split off from DLJ as a separate reporting entity. By the early 1970s, most of Alliance's commission business, which used to be quite profitable for DLJ, was being handed out to other firms for research and for liquidity. DLJ was precluded for fiduciary reasons from acting as a principal in transactions with its ERISA pension clients.

Out of all this emerged a rather distinct business strategy for DLJ, essentially contrarian to what others were doing until near the end of our first decade. By then we had a host of imitators, and it was time for another bold contrarian move—the decision to take DLJ public (never mind that it was against the rules of the NYSE) to raise new capital to meet the burgeoning liquidity needs of our institutional clients.

The key elements in this strategy, which have continued to guide the firm for 35 years, could be summarized as follows:

1. Concentrate on high-value-added products. Essentially we avoided commodity-type, me-too business.

2. Be a leader in all our activities. By inventing institutional research, we gained a strong leadership position in serving the emerging institutional markets. By pioneering the use of multiple managers of pension funds, we became the dominant securities firm in the asset management business (a lead that would still be maintained if Alliance Capital were a part of DLJ).

3. Concentrate on the high-end markets, institutional and corporate, and stay away from retail, the small individual investor market. I should add that my summer experience

(between the two years of Harvard Business School) as an order clerk in the Brooklyn branch of a large retail wire house forever cured me from wanting to serve small retail investors. I can only describe it as akin to Nathan Detroit's "floating crap game." When I graduated a year later from HBS I flew to the oak-paneled, clublike offices of Brown Brothers Harriman & Co. Incidentally, times change, and I think a much better case can be made today for the individual retail brokerage business. As corporations exit the pension business, individuals are being empowered to manage their own retirement funds. This has enormous implications for the future. This changed view on my part was at the heart of the new business strategy we developed later at Equitable—using our 7500 agents to concentrate on the savings and retirement needs of aging baby boomers.

4. Use superior research as our cutting edge, or key distinguishing feature of all we do. Just as Bill Donaldson thought we needed a raison d'être and Gypsy Rose Lee sang "You Gotta Have a Gimmick," I've always held to the original vision of DLJ as "The House That Research Built." The key underpinning of all, or almost all, DLJ business is research, including today's surging investment banking and merchant banking business. For a long time, the heart and soul of the firm was research. Even when we were too poor to afford a full complement of analysts, Ted Shen, the chief guardian of the research flame at DLJ over the years, evolved a "larger than life" strategy that allowed DLJ to retain the perception of being Number One in research against larger competition. Judging by DLJ's continued top rankings in research, which are better than ever, research is still a key element, though no longer the only one, in developing new business. Increasingly today, DLJ's skills in investment banking and in distribution are bringing in the new client relationships. But DLJ's key distinguishing feature vis-à-vis its competitors is still the firm's long-standing commitment to excellence in research.

5. Try to wear the "white hat" in all you undertake. There has always been a strong streak of idealism at DLJ, trying to do the "right things." Even though we were mavericks in literally

forcing public ownership on a reluctant NYSE, we thought it was the right thing—not just for DLJ, but for the entire industry and nation. Doing the right thing is considered good business at DLJ. But you should do the right thing regardless of whether or not it pays.

The reader might ask, after hearing about all these contrarian triumphs: "What did DLJ do wrong?" The answer is not much in the sixties—with one glaring exception that proved costly and forced the firm to play catch-up in the seventies. With all the firm's success in catching the initial wave of institutional brokerage and institutional money management in the sixties, we failed to use the prosperity and the firm's cachet to get into the investment banking business— that is to say the primary capital raising or underwriting side of Wall Street, an area that was almost moribund in the 1960s. All of DLJ's activities were in the so-called secondary market, buying and selling already existing securities. We were not in the business of raising new capital for companies in the 1960s. In part, this reflected a view held widely at DLJ that there was an inherent conflict of interest between advising corporations and being an impartial source of research for institutional investors. Beyond this idealistic view, the investment banking business simply didn't look like a very good business in the 1960s.

DLJ was founded in a period of capital surplus for U.S. corporations. The pressing need of corporations during the 1960s was not how to raise additional capital, but how to invest their excess cash flow. Even Morgan Stanley, the investment banking heir of J. P. Morgan, felt the pinch. Morgan Stanley was a partnership with no more than 300 employees and only $21 million in capital as the decade of the 1970s began. But the seventies turned out to be the reverse of the sixties. Capital was in great shortage after the Arab oil embargo crisis and the Fed's subsequent efforts to tighten credit to curb the rising inflation. The underwriting business DLJ had rejected in the sixties suddenly turned golden. To our dismay, we also discovered our institutional clients felt no qualms about listening to the investment advice emanating from the investment banking houses. The institutions saw it as a "buyer beware business" anyway and most had their own in-house research as a countercheck.

It was not that we didn't have our chance to leap into investment banking in a big way. We had several opportunities. Harriman Ripley & Co., the old-line investment banking arm of my alma mater Brown Brothers Harriman & Co. was up for grabs. I wanted to grab it, but my partners—not sharing my love of fine old names—turned it down. We also had a crack at Drexel, then a fine old name, on at least two occasions. But the jewel we really let get away was White, Weld & Co., a fine old firm that would have been a perfect cultural fit at DLJ, but ended up as part of Merrill Lynch.

Why did the firm miss these business opportunities, some of which literally came knocking on our door? Certainly a move into investment banking when the business was flat on its back in the late 1960s would have been contrarian. The answer really is hubris, which came from the firm's early successes. If we didn't invent it, it couldn't be very good. DLJ's failure to leverage its success in the secondary markets in the 1960s and get into the primary underwriting market led to inadequate profits and a game of catch-up for the next decade.

LEARNING FROM ADVERSITY

In looking back over my life and business career, it seems I always learned more from bad times or difficult experiences than I did from good times. This is probably the case for most of us—we remember the demanding schoolteacher or the difficult class where we were held to high standards of excellence. The experience may have been painful at the time, but it was rewarding and usually remembered gratefully later.

In this respect, the terrible 1970s were full of challenges that tested the very survival of DLJ, as well as my own self-esteem as a manager. We both survived, and I learned a lot from the experience. But even today it is difficult to be grateful for those ordeals, though they later served me extremely well in coping with The Equitable's problems in my second career there. I had begun to keep a diary on my fortieth birthday (in 1969), writing out a page or two of commentary each evening before bedtime (well, not *every* evening!). When I'm rested and "in control" my handwriting is usually small and fairly neat (a statement disputed by my secretary). Looking back at those pages from 1974, my handwriting had degenerated into an almost childlike scrawl, reflecting the intense pressure that I was under as the new CEO of DLJ. Even today, when I reread those pages of my diary, they still convey the horror of near failure.

What was so awful about the seventies? It is probably worth reviewing for those who have experienced only the almost continuously rising markets since then.

The decade began placidly enough, ushered in by DLJ's precedent-setting IPO in 1970, which forever changed the NYSE and financial community, though that was but dimly perceived at the time. Many market pundits and wags said it must surely be the top of the market when a *securities* firm was going public. They weren't far from wrong. The market almost immediately sold off, business activity slowed, and in 1970 DLJ had the embarrassment of reporting its first decline in earnings, ending 10 years of torrid growth, just as we came into public view. I remember writing the firm's annual report that year and describing the environment as being "like a dash of cold water, waking us up to the changing environment." Yet this was only a sample of what was to come.

We did pull ourselves together in 1971 and 1972, but got profitability back only to our pre-IPO level. The recovery, while tepid by DLJ's 1960 standards, was still sufficient for the American Express Company to decide it wanted to acquire DLJ in 1972. Bill Donaldson, who had become increasingly skeptical about the environment and was bone weary from the pressures of getting the firm public and managing it in a more competitive market, saw the advantages of such an alliance, but felt the decision should rest with the group. At the time, American Express also saw Bill Donaldson as an additional possible candidate in the "horse race" to succeed its CEO Howard Clark, who was nearing retirement. The entrepreneurial spirit of the rest of us at DLJ, especially Carl Tiedemann, our strong head of marketing, was such that we elected to sell only 25 percent, protecting our cultural independence while we were "getting to know" American Express. The honeymoon was brief. The cultures were totally different, and the high price American Express paid for its shares began to rankle when DLJ's subsequent results deteriorated and competitive pressures intensified as the markets began to weaken.

DLJ's IPO prospectus in 1970 had revealed for the first time the enormous profitability of the firm—50 percent gross profit margins on sales and an even higher return on equity. From that moment on, dozens of other securities firms sought to emulate DLJ's success in tapping the huge pot of fixed-rate commissions being generated by the increasingly active institutional investors. I should have recalled Brown Brothers' lesson of keeping one's profitability a secret.

Among the newcomers to the institutional markets in which DLJ dominated was Morgan Stanley, which surprisingly up until that point had no investment research, no trading, no distribution—just an old-school-tie-syndication of the "dirty work" of selling new issues, usually passed on to the socially less "white shoe" retail brokerage houses (like Dean Witter, which it is now embracing). Why Morgan Stanley didn't just suggest combining forces with DLJ, which had the best developed research and institutional distribution, is another one of those mysteries of life. We were both right there in the same building (140 Broadway), and it was the perfect complementary fit. Bill Donaldson was too independent to suggest it, and Bob Baldwin, Morgan Stanley's Chief, was most certainly too proud to think he couldn't do it better starting from scratch. Such were the beginnings of overcapacity on Wall Street, as we all began to invade one another's turf. Bob Baldwin should be given great credit, however, for shaking Morgan Stanley out of its lethargy.

Perhaps even more dangerous to DLJ's health than a bunch of imitators and new competitors were the envious eyes cast on our profitability by our institutional investor clients. Most seemed genuinely shocked by our high level of profitability, which was heavily keyed to the NYSE's structure of fixed-commission rates that forced them to pay the same fixed commission on big trades as on a 100-share purchase. The institutions complained they were tired of subsidizing the individual investor, as they put it. What they really meant was that they were tired of subsidizing Wall Street. Pressure began to mount at the SEC and in the media to force the NYSE to abandon its fixed commission rate structure and go to fully negotiated commission rates. When the SEC finally got around to ordering the Exchange to unfix rates in 1974, it was a case of the right long-term decision made at an abysmally bad time, as by then the deluge had hit Wall Street.

The stock market's problems began shortly after Richard Nixon's overwhelming reelection in late 1972—an event suitably celebrated by a last gasp of the bull market (eerily similar to circumstances following Bill Clinton's reelection in 1996?). The affairs of the nation then seemed to come to a halt, as the media and the populace wallowed in something called *Watergate*. This low-level break-in of the inept McGovern Presidential campaign headquarters escalated into a cause célèbre (which our European clients could never understand, so trivial did the event seem to be). Yet it undid the Nixon Presidency, which lapsed into paralysis. Watergate seemed to stir up all the passions of the Vietnam War, a war fought under two Democratic Administrations, which the luckless Nixon was actually in the process of bringing to a close.

All this might have been harmless, even amusing intramural warfare between Democrats and Republicans had not disaster hit in the form of the Arab-Israeli war, which broke out in 1973. In retaliation for U.S. support of Israel, the Arab nations moved to blockade the Middle East oil exports and effectively nationalized the interests of U.S., British, and other oil companies in the region. The nation that 20 years later would preclude Saddam Hussein from seizing Kuwait's oil this time "let them get away with it." Nixon was so weakened by Watergate and Vietnam that he and the nation stood by helplessly and did nothing. It was an object lesson on the dangers of a weakened Chief Executive. As far as I can tell, it was also the greatest transfer of wealth in the history of the world.

Even today, I hear politicians and economists wondering what went wrong in the mid-1970s that led to such a drastic reduction in U.S. prosperity. The answer always seemed so simple to me. We allowed literally trillions of dollars of future oil revenues to be transferred to Arab oil coffers, away from U.S. and British corporate treasuries at Exxon, Texaco, Mobil, etc. We haven't been the same since then.

The resulting flow of Arab petrodollars, as we called them, were not immediately disruptive to world economies because the Arabs, led by the Saudis, prudently redeposited them in U.S. banks (with the effective guarantee of the U.S. Treasury). The resulting huge inflow of dollars into the major U.S. banks as deposits eased the pain and negated some of the outrage or criticism that might otherwise have been forthcoming. Because the Federal Reserve had raised interest rates to double-digit levels to offset the inflation of oil prices, which leapt from $4 a barrel to $40 a barrel, we also found ourselves paying dearly in high interest rates to get the money back. Completing the almost Greek tragedy for the developed Western nations, U.S. banks were then encouraged to recycle the huge inflow of petrodollars to developing nations, especially in Latin America. The resulting bad loans, which became evident several years later, further extinguished American wealth.

The consequences of the above sequence of events were devastating for the stock and bond markets, as double-digit interest rates demolished both. Into this cauldron, the SEC plowed right ahead with its plan to unfix commission rates, which immediately fell from 40 cents a share to 10 cents (more like 4 cents a share on average today). Trading activity (or portfolio turnover at institutions) also came to a virtual halt, dropping all the way back to the low levels prevailing when DLJ was founded 14 years earlier.

A quick anecdote:

Shortly before these catastrophic events flattened Wall Street, I had succeeded in luring my old HBS classmate John Chalsty to join DLJ. John had been with Exxon, formerly Standard Oil of New Jersey, when I ran into him on the streets of London. At the time, we were looking for an oil analyst at DLJ. A light flashed on—why not John Chalsty? I proceeded to offer the job to John, with this come-on: "Why don't you come to Wall Street and get rich and have some fun?" A year later, oil prices had gone up from $4 a barrel to $40, while brokerage commission rates on the NYSE had collapsed from 40 cents a share to—eventually—4 cents a share. Chalsty realized he had been whipsawed—the oil companies were coining money while we were starving. John used to kid me about my promise of his becoming rich and having fun on Wall Street. "Dick, if you'd been right on one of the two, it wouldn't have been so bad!" John stuck it out, though, and 20 years later he *has* made a lot of money and he *has* had a lot of fun. But back to our scary crisis in 1974....

How we survived that horrible year, my first as CEO, still remains something of a miracle to me. How many businesses could survive a 75 percent drop in their selling price at the same time their unit volume was plunging? Certainly without DLJ's IPO and infusion of capital in 1970, it would have been impossible for the firm to survive. But added to that we had our own internal management crisis that inhibited coping with the difficult environment.

I had become heir to the mantel of chief executive officer of DLJ at the end of 1973—talk about a baptism of fire in 1974! Bill Donaldson, whose dream had always been public ownership for DLJ, told me he felt burned out and in need of "repotting" in 1973 when he was approached by Henry Kissinger to become undersecretary of state. It sounded like a dream opportunity for public service to Donaldson, who had always contemplated a second career in the public sector. Kissinger at that time was about to embark on his shuttle diplomacy to resolve Arab-Israeli differences. At the time, I didn't believe Donaldson realized just how bad things were about to get on Wall Street, nor did I. Even he admitted the business was no fun anymore—and under DLJ's eighth corporate objective, it had to be fun. So off he went to Washington, for what turned out to be an equally "unfun" experience as Kissinger's deputy in the collapsing Nixon Administration.

Dan Lufkin had left the firm in 1971, shortly after DLJ's IPO in early 1970. In many ways, his interest in the firm had begun to wane in the late sixties as we became larger and no longer exclusively focused on the small growth companies he loved. He stuck around like a good trooper to provide a united front for the trail-blazing DLJ IPO but resigned a year later. Long interested in the environment, he became one of the key organizers of the first Earth Day. He became Connecticut's first Commissioner of Environmental Protection and considered (but decided against) a run for the governorship of Connecticut.

As the world came crashing around my ears in mid-1974, Lufkin called from Connecticut to say "Bear, I think you need help." To this I readily assented and consented that Dan would return as co-chief executive officer.

Deliver me from such a fate (co-chief executives) ever again—even with a good friend. It soon became apparent that

Dan had totally different views as to an appropriate business strategy for DLJ. He was much more bearish than I (despite my nickname). Dan felt, with some justification, that things had altered permanently. He favored a sharp contraction in the size of the firm, refocusing it on investing in small and developing growth companies. I saw 1974 more in cyclical terms. As Bud Newquist would have said—the worse things get, the bigger the recovery. I felt strongly that better times were ahead and that we should sail on ("hang on" is probably a better description!), keeping our highly respected research team intact, continuing to build our successful money management business (which became Alliance Capital), and expanding into some areas of fixed income (with interest rates so high bonds were extraordinary buys). Our views, in short, were diametrically opposed.

Dan ultimately solved the dilemma by voluntarily withdrawing from the contest of wills. While on the surface it appears my view was correct, since times did quickly improve and DLJ is still alive and well, I would be the first to acknowledge it is entirely possible that the firm could also have done well had it contracted in size, raised new capital, and concentrated solely on investing in small growth companies, which has always been Dan Lufkin's forte. As Dan pointed out to me, Kohlberg, Kravis & Roberts was formed a year later with a similar strategy and obviously has been enormously successful. Despite the strong disagreement over strategy, Dan and I remained friends, perhaps because we are both contrarians. With hindsight either strategy would have worked (an example of why Harvard Business School cases never have a single "school solution" to the problem). Things were so depressed at the time that almost anything that kept you in business would have paid off handsomely. It was not a time to quit.

The bad news was that this rupture left a badly weakened chief executive—me—lacking a clear consensus as to the right course of action. I was surrounded by a number of strong chieftains, each of whom was probably as capable as I to head the firm. We were all badly shaken by the firm's loss in 1974 and each had strong opinions. The compromise solution was a bad one: band together and form an "office of the chief executive." If co-chief executives didn't work, with hindsight, there was very little reason to believe *five* co-chief executives would work, which was about what the office of the chief executive amounted to. And so there was still discontent and uncertainty as to who had the right vision.

Things ultimately did get better, but not until I had gotten my own team in place. Curiously, American Express helped in the process by deciding to spin off its 25 percent ownership of DLJ to its shareholders. Spinning us off, rather than selling DLJ at a loss, was a clever way to avoid running a very big loss through American Express's income statement. By then, the market value of the investment was small and insignificant and frankly an embarrassment to American Express. Howard Clark, the very capable CEO of American Express, had also been disappointed by Bill Donaldson's departure for Washington, although he concurred with Bill's decision at the time. I remember Howard's words when I was summoned to his office, "Dick, don't take this personally—we think you're a nice guy—but this investment just doesn't make any sense for us now." He then presented me with a fait accompli: they had already decided to spin DLJ off to their shareholders. I was never asked my opinion on the matter.

Even though I liked the people at American Express, I felt strangely emancipated when I walked out of that office. Their large block of stock actually had been adding to management instability, since they felt no particular loyalty to me or any of us for that matter. In retrospect, this was another chance to turn a problem into an opportunity.

Subsequently, when the DLJ shares were spun off to American Express's unsuspecting shareholders, most of them not surprisingly elected to sell. DLJ's shares, which had been bought by American Express at $15, briefly fell below $2 a share, such was the pessimism rampant at the time. I recall a DLJ Christmas party about that time at which we were so poor we had a cash bar. A glass of scotch cost $2, which everyone joked was equal to one share of DLJ stock. The same shares, incidentally, were bought by The Equitable Life Assurance Society at $30 a share a decade later.

In this environment, my white knight emerged in the form of a shrewd Saudi Arabian businessman, Suliman Olayan, whom I had befriended years previously—even before the big run up in oil prices. By coincidence, Suliman had scheduled a dinner with me on that fateful day American Express announced its spin-off of DLJ to its shareholders. I told him at the time that I expected DLJ stock would collapse under the pressure of so much selling and that it would be literally given away. Suliman's reply was to give me an unlimited buy order for DLJ stock. And so for the next few months we bought and bought, never forcing the stock up but waiting for it to come in as the American Express shareholders individually decided to sell. Ultimately, Olayan and his then-partner Prince Khalid Bin Abdullah Bin Abdulrahman Al Saud, a brother of the King of Saudi Arabia, ended up with a 25 percent ownership in DLJ, acquired at bargain prices.

With a strong supporter in the Olayan Group and the removal of the American Express block, I was able, at last, to consolidate my position as CEO and pursue the strategy that I felt was right for the firm and get my own team in place. It came almost as a relief to everyone in the firm to have the bickering ended, and someone at the helm who could make decisions and enforce them. In my experience, *uncertainty about who is the boss is the greatest cause of corporate failure.*

The foregoing experiences should explain why I titled this chapter "Learning from Adversity," so let me try to summarize the key lessons I learned.

1. *Co-Chairmen Equal No Chairmen.*   Even with a good friend like Dan Lufkin and mutual respect, there has to be one boss—one place where the buck stops. Dan's strategy might have worked just as well as mine over the long term, but the point is that we were canceling one another out. Far too much time was spent in debate, and the professional staff was forced into the position of having to choose sides.

2. *Never Form an "Office of the Chief Executive Officer"*   or any other such entity. This is a sure sign of a house divided and signals a weak CEO. I tried it briefly and it was a disaster.

Such arrangements inevitably are a sop to the egos of rival chieftains who are jealous of one another. As an investor, if I see a company set up an "office of the chief executive," I run for the hills. It's a sure sign of internal divisions and coming strife. Just why some consultants continue to recommend such structures, which preclude a strong CEO, are beyond me.

3. *Get Your Own Team in Place.*   There is no more important piece of advice that I can give to a new chief executive than to urge the absolute necessity of getting your own team in place (you also have to get rid of the old team or you will still have infighting). Until I was able to consolidate control, we were working at cross purposes. Some of the executives I inherited undoubtedly thought they were more qualified than I to run the Company (and this might have been true—after all I had always advocated hiring someone smarter than yourself). But there was a crying need to come together, under one banner, one leader. If your key supporting executives are either expecting or hoping that you will fail as CEO, there is a high probability that that will be precisely the outcome.

Getting your own team in place is easier said than done. Frequently the new CEO either lacks the power or is unwilling to make draconian changes in existing senior management, at least until some discreet interval or trial-and-error period has passed. At DLJ, I was not able to consolidate my authority as CEO until the wild card of American Express's large 25 percent block had been resolved and substantial ownership had shifted to investors who strongly backed me as CEO.

I would not pretend to tell a new CEO how to go about "cleaning house" when there is no clear consensus for such a move. Each situation is different. But it has to be done sooner or later, the sooner the better. Otherwise, office politics will go on and on, eventually grinding down the authority of the CEO and leading to corporate paralysis.

4. *Surround Yourself with People Who Complement Your Strengths and Weaknesses.*   That's complement with an *e*, not an *i!* The *worst* thing you can do in getting your own team in place is to try to clone yourself with think-alike, act-alike, look-alike types. There is an almost irresistible temptation to do so. It's so comfortable. If you are a marketing/sales-oriented type of CEO, for example, it is vital to surround yourself with some key people with strong financial analytical skills. When I became CEO of DLJ, I was perceived as perhaps too much of an optimist who might not be tough enough in cutting costs and as hard-nosed as the difficult times seemed to demand. The jury was out, so to speak, on my ability to manage the company. My answer was to promote two of DLJ's younger executives who had reputations for disciplined thinking and rigorous financial analysis. These two—John Castle and Dick Pechter—over the years were invaluable to me in helping steer a course between building the financial "Camelot" of my dreams and the harsh realities of the marketplace (of which they constantly reminded me).

Starting in 1977, DLJ went on to put together a string of 28 consecutive quarters in which earnings exceeded the prior year. DLJ's merchant banking group, under Castle's disciplined approach, contributed importantly to this record through timely capital gains at critical junctures. While I always have felt elaborate business plans and action steps, so enamored by management consultants, bordered on being a waste of time (they are so hypothetical and theoretical), Castle and Pechter—both Harvard Business School Baker Scholars— made sure we always had in place a business plan that would have earned "high distinction" from the best McKinsey consultant. The presence of Castle and Pechter in my managerial lineup served to alleviate internal and external concerns that I might be too easygoing—a perception that has always followed me until recent years. Interestingly, it's a perception that has allowed me to keep the goodwill of my associates as the "good guy" and also to get away with making a series of difficult and unpleasant decisions, which nevertheless had to be made. If you are perceived to be "soft," I found you can turn even this handicap to your advantage. Keep thinking how to turn problems into opportunities!

5. *Do Your Own Strategizing.*   I could never understand why any manager worth his salt would want to bring in a consultant to set business policy. Yet Dan Lufkin, whom I greatly respect, insisted on doing this when he returned to DLJ in 1974 at the height of our disarray. Since Dan and I were thinking in diametrically opposite directions at the time, I suppose his purpose in bringing in the consultant was to validate his point of view. All too often that's the real reason consultants are brought in, to validate someone's previously held views. I will never forget their advice—get back to your "core" business (how consultants love that term, more recently elevated to "core competence"). Our core competence was said to be institutional research and brokerage. That business turned out to be moribund for at least the next decade as the old fixed commission rate system continued to crumble. Worst of all they advised selling Alliance Capital, our thriving money management company which was not supposed to be core. Someone conveniently offered $1 million cash and $5 million in paper shortly thereafter for Alliance. Ultimately, I stopped this freight train of a bad idea—but it is not easy after the cat gets out of the bag. Today Alliance has a market value of over $2.5 billion. Fundamentally, as CEO, you must fashion your own vision of the future. In this I don't believe consultants can be of much help. If you need them to set strategy, you are the wrong person to be CEO.

6. *Use Bad Times to Expand.*   This tenet of my contrarian philosophy was borne of DLJ's experience in the late 1970s, when times were universally tough on Wall Street. In 1977 we acquired Pershing & Company, a private partnership providing order executions and securities clearance services to an elite network of the top regional securities firms. Pershing's partners, aging and faced with further investment in new computers, elected to sell to DLJ at what was essentially book value. The company had enormous hidden assets, including 23 seats on the NYSE which were extraordinarily depressed in market value at the time. Pershing, which was acquired for $7 million, now returns its purchase price in earnings almost every month! Since at the time we lacked the cash to buy it, we simultaneously acquired Wood, Struthers & Winthrop, a relatively cash-rich old-line investment firm whose partners were willing to take DLJ stock. We used the cash to buy out the Pershing partners, and at the same time we gained an interesting investment counsel franchise in Wood, Struthers' money management business.

Over the years, DLJ has continued to use this philosophy of expanding in bad times. More frequently in recent years, the firm, under John Chalsty's leadership, has used hard times as hiring opportunities, corralling new talent as former leading firms such as Drexel and Kidder Peabody were liquidated or taken over by others.

EPILOGUE ON
DLJ AND ALLIANCE

The most important lesson I learned at DLJ was not from adversity but rather from prosperity. The lesson is the importance of hiring really bright people. You empower them and then they make *you* look good. Exhibits A and B for me in this period were John Chalsty, who has been CEO of DLJ for the past 11 years, and Dave Williams, who has led Alliance Capital (DLJ's original money management arm) for nearly 20 years. Both are superb managers, still going strong.

John Chalsty entered my life more than 40 years ago, when we both matriculated to the Harvard Business School. At the time I was President of a party-giving group of Southerners at HBS called the Southern Club. Chalsty persuaded us that, as a native of South Africa, he qualified for membership as being the Southernmost Southerner at HBS. John, who is perhaps the most articulate person I have ever known (rivaled only by George Gould, another early DLJ-er who later became Under Secretary of Treasury), went on to achieve Baker Scholar status, ranking in the top 1 percent of his class at HBS. He did not join DLJ until six years later following that fateful encounter with me in London when I lured him to Wall Street just in time for the crash of 1974.

Chalsty became CEO of DLJ in mid-1986, following the departure of John Castle. In that year, DLJ had gross revenues of $600 million and pretax operating profits of only $70 million. Alliance Capital, which previously had been part of DLJ and had accounted for almost half the firm's profits, was separated from DLJ at the time of our deal with Equitable. Thereafter Alliance became a separate reporting subsidiary of The Equitable, which owned 100 percent of both entities. While the split up was painful to me (I had been instrumental in starting both and had fought hard to keep Alliance as part of the family), it had some beneficial effects. DLJ, which had always been rather different from other securities firms because of its large asset management operations, now had to get deadly serious about developing its investment banking business. Necessity is the mother of invention.

John Chalsty, prior to his ascendancy to the CEO role at DLJ, had headed investment banking. In moving up to CEO he was fortunate in having Joe Roby, a feisty and thoroughly professional investment banker, on hand to take over as head of investment banking. Roby, a Harvard Business School graduate who, as previously mentioned, came to DLJ via Kidder Peabody, proved to be a fiery leader working together with Chalsty in marshaling the firm's resources.

What a difference a decade made! By 1996, DLJ's total revenues had grown to $3.5 billion with pretax operating profits of $474 million (despite the separation of Alliance Capital). Interestingly, in line with DLJ's strategy of sticking to high-end markets, revenues per employee were about three times the industry average and nearly double those of Morgan Stanley and Goldman Sachs, DLJ's high-end competitors.

The key driver—though not the only success story—was investment banking. Incredibly, DLJ vaulted to fourth place from seventeenth, trailing only Merrill Lynch, Goldman Sachs, and Morgan Stanley, in total underwriting revenues in 1995, and to prove it was no fluke, in 1996. Investment banking accounted for about half of DLJ's total profitability. In fixed income DLJ challenged the popular late-1980s wisdom (post-Drexel) that the high-yield bond business was dead. Buttressed by an aggressive hiring program after the 1987 stock market crash, the firm built a highly profitable, number-one ranked high-yield bond practice. Meanwhile DLJ continued its leadership in its original institutional equities business, ranking number one or two worldwide on a consistent basis.

Pershing, which had been bought for only $7 million in 1977, 19 years later had operating profits of $100 million.

What form of alchemy did DLJ use to vault from virtually nothing in investment banking a decade ago to the fourth-ranked position on Wall Street in 1995 and 1996? Partly it was a canny mix of the use of capital (DLJ's own and that of its officers) in making direct merchant banking investments in corporations in tandem with a bridge loan fund provided by Equitable that allowed DLJ to provide interim financing to prospective corporate clients. The bridge loan fund was enormously successful, avoiding so-called hung bridges (loans that could not be paid at maturity), thanks both to the good credit analysis and greatly expanded distribution capacity of the firm. This included the number-one ranked high-yield bond group and other fixed income groups as well as the firm's enhanced ability to distribute new equity offerings to high net worth individuals as well as institutions. This unique blend of merchant banking and investment banking capability, together with the "can do, give the enemy no quarter" attitude fostered by Chalsty, Roby, and their key associates carried the day. In the end, it turned out DLJ didn't have to acquire an old-line investment banking firm in order to be successful.

Things came full circle for DLJ in late 1995 when the company that invented public ownership for New York Stock Exchange member firms went public again. Through a combination of sales of new stock to 1500 DLJ professionals and a public offering of new shares, Equitable's ownership of DLJ was reduced to 80 percent (actually 73 percent on a fully converted, fully diluted basis). Recent prices of the shares, again listed on the NYSE, valued DLJ at $3.8 billion.

Alliance, under Dave Williams's inspired leadership, has had equally spectacular growth. When Dave took charge in 1977, following our decision not to sell Alliance, assets under management totaled $7 billion and operations were essentially at breakeven. Some 20 years later, assets under management now total $183 billion and operating profits were $193 million in 1996. Alliance, which was partially taken public in 1988, now has a quoted market value in excess of $2 billion recently.

Equitable owns 60 percent, with management and the public owning the rest.

Dave Williams made several key decisions along the way that totally changed the character of Alliance, which originally had managed only U.S. corporate pension funds. Most critical was a decision to enter the mutual fund business. Led by John Carifa, now president, who pioneered Alliance's entry into this arena, Alliance now has more than $75 billion of mutual funds under management. Alliance has also gone global with 10 percent of the firm's assets under management sourced overseas and another 15 percent invested overseas. Alliance also has diversified its once nearly complete dependence on the stock market, and today over half the assets under management are fixed income. Finally, Alliance has taken over the management of Equitable's own portfolio of investments, adding nearly $50 billion to assets under management. Despite all this growth, investment performance has continued to be superior, led by vice chairmen Bruce Calvert and Alfred Harrison. Harrison's $15 billion "large growth stock" portfolio ranks in the top 1 percent of this investment category over its 18-year span.

Interestingly (at least to me, as the godfather of both), DLJ together with Alliance had combined pretax operating earnings of nearly $700 million in 1996 on revenues of $4 billion. This is after large bonuses to the people who would have been partners had DLJ and Alliance been structured as a private partnership such as Goldman Sachs. The combined market value exceeds $6 billion. This represents more than a fifteenfold increase in value over what Equitable paid for DLJ 12 years ago—an increase in value that was critical to saving The Equitable. And for those of us who were around at DLJ's humble beginning with our tiny $100,000 equity base, the progress has been mind-boggling. Messrs. Donaldson, Lufkin & Jenrette are very proud of their successors. DLJ and Alliance get better and better each year. The tradition of hiring someone smarter than yourself has been passed on to a new generation.

PART TWO

A SECOND BUSINESS CAREER

The second defining experience of my business career was the antithesis of the essentially entrepreneurial experience of starting DLJ from scratch, then nursing it through some bad times before the sun came out again. The Equitable experience was totally different. It involved a 140-year-old mutual life insurance company, which had been a great growth enterprise in the last half of the nineteenth century (becoming the world's largest life insurance company by the turn of the twentieth century), but which had gradually become staid and bureaucratic after the death in 1899 of its dynamic founder, Henry Hyde. Hyde had the ability to cut through red tape. His successors, for the most part, did not. Equitable, like most of the major mutuals, had gradually lost prestige and influence, losing market share at various times to the banks, securities firms, and money management mutual fund companies during the post-World War II period.

Well-intentioned efforts by Equitable to shake this lethargy in the 1980s, such as the successful DLJ acquisition, led to overexpansion. There were too many new ventures, a costly and excessive exposure to guaranteed investment contracts, which nearly sank the company, and an aggressive investment posture that worked well for a while but backfired in the early 1990s as U.S. real estate values plummeted. The inability of the company to raise outside equity capital, because of the mutual ownership structure, was a key weakness.

This is the story of how I, and DLJ, became intimately involved in this saga and the ultimately successful rescue of this former grande dame of American finance from financial collapse.

CHAPTER
NINE

THE EQUITABLE
EXPERIENCE

The Equitable Life Assurance Society of the United States,
a large and venerable mutual (policyholder-owned) life
insurance company, acquired 100 percent of the stock of DLJ
in early 1985, roughly a decade after the trauma of 1974,
which had been so painful. The memory of that year lingered
on in my mind, despite the 28 consecutive quarters of year-
over-year gains in earnings for DLJ after 1977.

Times were again changing. The Glass-Steagall legislation,
formulated during the Depression of the 1930s to separate
commercial banking from the perceived conflicts of investment banking, appeared to be on its last legs (surprisingly it
still exists today, albeit badly frayed). Financial deregulation
seemed to be the way of the future during the Reagan years in
the 1980s, and it was widely predicted that banks, insurance
companies, and securities firms would all end up under one
corporate umbrella. During this time, publicly owned DLJ had
to fend off at least one hostile suitor—Primerica, then led by
Jerry Tsai, who had been one of DLJ's best customers (at
Fidelity) in our early years. Meanwhile our Saudi investors, or
at least some of their managers, were manifesting some rest-
lessness. Wasn't this the right time to cash in?

In this environment, I was introduced to the amiable John
Carter, Equitable's president and chief executive officer. The
occasion of our get-together was a hearing on Glass Steagall,
conducted by Senator Tim Wirth of Colorado (later we kidded
Tim that he never got a finder's fee for our deal that came out
of this hearing). Carter and I were paired on the side of those

opposed to letting banks get into the insurance business or into the securities industry (at the time I was chairman of The Securities Industry Association, ipso facto making me the chief defender of the industry against incursions by the vastly better-capitalized banks). To make a long story short, John and I felt we beat up our bank opponents rather badly in the debate. We felt that we made a good team. Carter, a Yale and Harvard Business School graduate, seemed a familiar type to me.

In our heart of hearts, both Carter and I shared the view that eventually the banks would get access to both industries, insurance and securities. But meanwhile, since there was no law precluding an insurance company from owning a securities company, why not get a jump on the banks by combining forces?

Not everyone at DLJ was enthusiastic about the idea. John Castle, for one, preferred to remain independent, and a year later he left to form his own company (Castle, Harlan), with another DLJ alumnus Len Harlan. While Castle might have been just what was needed to shake up what turned out to be a lethargic Equitable, he undoubtedly fared better financially by going his own way and forming a leveraged buyout firm.

In any event, the pressures to do the deal were overwhelming. The price Equitable offered for DLJ seemed right: two times book value, which on Wall Street is usually viewed as the time to sell, especially since our stock had traded at a discount to book value for much of the prior decade. Equitable also made the usual prenuptial promises of independence for DLJ—surprisingly they were honored. Most importantly, and erroneously, Equitable (with $40 billion in assets and a double-A credit rating at the time) was perceived at DLJ as a "deep pocket" in the event we needed more capital. Apparently we didn't do our homework very well, since some of Equitable's coming problems were already visible. But the offer of $440 million for our stock was all cash, which perhaps lulled us into complacency. No one dreamed that a great American icon like The Equitable Life Assurance Society could get into serious financial difficulty.

Although I never intended to remain at Equitable more than a year or so to insure an orderly transition for DLJ and

Alliance to new ownership, one thing led to another; there always seemed to be a good reason to hang on. While remaining chairman of DLJ, I was invited to become a vice chairman and director of Equitable in 1985. A couple of years later when Leo Walsh, Carter's top deputy, ascended to the role of chief operating officer, I was asked to take over his role of watching over all the investment subsidiaries. These included DLJ, Alliance, Equitable Capital and Equitable Real Estate, as well as sundry other financial service companies that The Equitable had acquired in prior years, most of which I eventually merged into other Equitable subsidiaries or sold off. I was next given the role of chief investment officer, succeeding Walsh in this role. When Bob Froehlke, the nonexecutive chairman, retired in 1989, I was asked to become chairman of the board. In this I was apparently a second choice—Carter had hoped to take over the chairmanship himself, retaining the chief executive officer role and promoting Leo Walsh to president and chief operating officer. Probably because of Walsh's association with the looming problems in Equitable's huge block of guaranteed interest contracts, key directors balked. I was available as a compromise chairman—at age 60 not too threatening to anyone. Leo Walsh took early retirement, which was a disappointment to him, but probably the best thing that ever happened to him. Like John Castle, he struck gold in the LBO market and was spared the agony that was ahead at Equitable.

Despite all these high-sounding titles that were handed to me, I never felt that I had become a complete confidante or partner of John Carter. I was always viewed as an outsider. Despite our initial feelings that we made a good team, there were some awkward aspects to my relationship with Carter. For starters, I was older than John by seven years. More importantly, someone seemed to have persuaded John, or maybe he persuaded himself, that I secretly aspired to his job as CEO. Nothing could have been further from the truth—a big sprawling organization like Equitable was not my dish of tea.

I also saw the problems coming and tried hard to convince John that he had to take draconian action before the roof caved in. After a banner investment year in 1988, when everything went right in Equitable's aggressively invested portfolio, I tried hard to convince John to merge The Equitable with Metropolitan Life, the second largest U.S. insurer that had a triple-A credit rating at the time. Met Life was receptive to the idea. The merger would have created a colossus, the largest U.S. life insurance company, bigger than Prudential, with more than $200 billion assets under management. The companies were complementary in other ways, including distribution, where Met Life was investing heavily (and not so successfully) to get into the upscale life insurance markets and where Equitable already had great strength. In the end, Carter was dissatisfied that Met Life executives would have gained most of the senior management positions in the combined company. He aborted the discussions on the grounds that it would have been the end of the "Equitable culture."

What were the problems afflicting Equitable and what was the culture that John Carter sought to protect?

The culture of The Equitable was that of an old-line mutual life insurer—part paternalistic, part bureaucratic. The company also had a reputation for being sales driven, and it was often referred to as "the agents' company." Committee meetings of home office executives ran on endlessly, making it difficult to pinpoint responsibility when something went wrong. Internally, the company was referred to as "Mother Equitable," and in speaking to employees, John Carter liked to refer to "The Equitable Family."

Because of the peculiar diffused nature of policyholder ownership, management was free from the usual nagging complaints of shareholders and analysts about profitability, or lack thereof. When there were complaints, they usually came from the agency field force if a product was not "competitive." The major credit rating agencies, other than A.M. Best, never even bothered to rate the large mutual life insurers like Equitable until the early 1980s, such was the mutuals' mystique for financial probity. No wonder Carter once boasted in a speech at DLJ that "you are looking at the most secure CEO you'll ever see." At the time I thought that was tempting fate.

To his credit John Carter, a loyal son of Harvard Business School, *tried* to make the culture of The Equitable more profit-oriented. The main thrust of his administration was decentralization, or "downstreaming new subsidiaries out of the old Equitable monolith," as he preferred to call the process. "Downstreaming" had some benefits in creating a more entrepreneurial culture, but ultimately it led to many expensive, overlapping layers of management. The new subsidiaries also had ravenous appetites for capital, which Equitable had no way of meeting as a mutual owned by its policyholders. At heart Carter was a marketing person who trusted outside consultants and a few close internal confidantes to take care of the financial side of the business. I suspect it was a case of no one wanting to be the bearer of bad news.

Whatever the reason, Equitable's capital base had not kept up with the company's sales and liability growth. The new lines of business, including a health-care company, a leasing company, a Japanese life insurance company, and two new insurance subsidiaries selling annuities through alternative channels, all carried enormous surplus strain (insurance terminology for capital requirements) as start-ups. Someone (probably the consultants) had grossly miscalculated Equitable's capacity to finance these ambitious new lines of activity. To make up for the shortfall Equitable began to rely increasingly on something called *surplus relief,* which sounded to me like a new headache remedy. In reality, it was nothing more than a quick fix, since it had to be paid back out of future earnings. Meanwhile other ominous clouds appeared on the horizon as the regulators began to talk of new, more stringent capital requirements for life insurers, which Equitable would be hard put to meet.

The biggest problem gnawing away at the company's financial base, however, was Equitable's huge $15 billion block of guaranteed investment contracts (GICs). There was a growing negative spread between the interest Equitable had committed to pay on these contracts versus the investment income being earned on the assets underlying the contracts. These contracts, essentially debt obligations, had been sold by Equitable to U.S. pension funds as funding vehicles. They guaranteed a fixed rate of interest over long periods of time. In reality, the effect was to greatly leverage The Equitable's balance sheet, although no one seemed to think of it in that light. Equitable had literally invented the GIC in the late 1970s as a means of maintaining a presence in the huge U.S. pension fund market. The product had been widely emulated by other insurers, eager to regain a share of the pension fund market that had been lost to the banks. Equitable was the nation's largest issuer of GICs in the mid-1980s.

In and of itself, the GIC might not have been a bad product had it been possible to match up the maturities of the assets and liabilities. This would have allowed the company to lock in a positive spread between the higher rates it expected to earn on these assets above what it was obligated to pay in interest on the GICs. The Equitable contract, however, proved to be flawed in that it contained provisions that, in effect, allowed the purchaser of the GIC to obtain a higher rate of interest if interest rates rose. This was equivalent to the old cardinal sin of borrowing short and lending long. When interest rates subsequently rose, Equitable was forced to ratchet up the rates it was paying to competitive levels in order to keep the money in place. The long maturity bonds that had been purchased to match the GIC liabilities fell sharply in value as interest rates rose, precluding the alternative of simply selling them and paying off the GIC rather than extending it at the new higher rates. Because of the weakness in the bond markets, on a mark-to-market basis The Equitable's capital would have been wiped out if the bonds had to be sold. So Equitable was forced to renegotiate the GICs at ever higher rates in order to keep the funds in place. DuPont, for example, was able to obtain a $17\frac{3}{4}$ percent interest rate from Equitable when it rolled over a large GIC for its Conoco subsidiary on December 31, 1981. Over the next 6 years, funds invested for Conoco at this extraordinarily high rate rose to $400 million.

The reverse was not true when interest rates subsequently fell. The pension funds that bought Equitable's GICs could continue to enjoy the high interest rates guaranteed in the contract throughout the maturity of the GIC. Thus, as interest rates fell in the post-1981 deflationary environment, obviously no one cashed in their GICs. To make matters even worse, many GIC buyers like DuPont had contractual rights to invest more pension cash flow with The Equitable at the high rates prevailing at the time the contract was issued. At this point Equitable was in the equally untenable position of having borrowed "long," at high fixed rates, and invested "short" at a time when interest rates were falling and corporations began to repay the high-coupon bonds that Equitable had bought to back the GICs. At the new lower level of interest rates, it was impossible for Equitable to reinvest these funds at comparable rates, short of markedly reducing the quality of its portfolio and assuming more risk. It was a looming disaster.

Faced with the likelihood of a widening gap between the fixed rate of interest that the company was contractually obligated to pay on the GICs and the much lower projected income on the bonds and other assets backing the GICs, the only solution, other than prayer, seemed to lie in a more aggressive investment approach in an attempt to generate more income—in effect to try to "invest our way out of the problem." This meant taking on more risk. Often this results in digging an even deeper hole, which proved to be partly the case this time.

Equitable, which had been burned badly by inflation in the 1970s, already had above-average exposure to equity real estate, which with hindsight seems risky. This was supplemented by something called *enhanced return investments,* essentially high-yield bonds (aka junk bonds), sometimes with equity kickers. Over the years, they actually worked out quite well for Equitable, except briefly during a critical moment in the early 1990s when there were some defaults and literally no resale market for the bonds. Equitable's large investments in DLJ, Alliance, and the other investment subsidiaries also were perceived by regulators and rating agencies to be aggressive, somewhat risky equity investments. Fortunately, these turned out to be a financial bonanza for Equitable.

The key assumption behind many of The Equitable's investments, especially equity real estate, was that inflation would continue at a high rate. Investment grade bonds obviously flunked that test, and so Equitable held relatively less of this category of investments than did its less aggressive, more cautious competitors. When I first came to Equitable, I was surprised to find that every investment coming before the Investment Committee had to disclose if and how the investment was "inflation adaptive." Alas, the company was fighting last year's war. There was relatively low inflation thereafter.

The aggressive investment policy worked well, for a while. Despite the decline in market rates of interest, Equitable earned more than 10 percent on its General Account investments in 1988, one of the highest in the life insurance industry that year. The bad news was that the imbedded rate of interest Equitable was paying on the GICs still exceeded 12 percent. The resulting negative spread of 200 basis points on nearly $15 billion of GICs resulted in a "locked in" operating loss of $300 million annually until this block of business matured. But the roof did not cave in on The Equitable that year because the high portfolio yield resulted in large profits in the rest of Equitable's businesses, offsetting the GIC losses. DLJ and Alliance also performed well, earning a high rate of return on Equitable's investment.

After 1988, the capital markets began to tremble as the Fed once again moved to tighten credit and rein in the threat of renewed inflation. Still by dint of realizing large capital gains on sales of old real estate (with a low cost basis) in 1989, Equitable once again managed to keep the wolf away from the door.

Thereafter, it was all downhill. As Mike Milken's junk bond empire and Drexel Burnham Lambert began to crumble in the fall of 1989, the die was cast. Junk bond prices collapsed in the secondary trading markets. Executive Life, which had been rated triple A by one leading rating agency because of its strong capital position, later collapsed by virtue of having almost all of its assets in junk bonds, for which there was temporarily no market. Since Equitable had one of the highest percentages of junk bonds (10 percent) outside of Executive Life, the credit-rating agencies began to express alarm, especially given the company's low percentage of capital to liabilities.

Junk bonds weren't the only problem facing The Equitable. By 1990 the real estate markets had turned sour. Virtually all of the old capital gains in the real estate portfolio had been "harvested," an internal euphemism for living off past unrealized gains. Equitable's strategy of aggressive investing, which had worked well for the past seven years in helping mitigate the GIC losses, suddenly exacerbated the problem.

What to do? With the wolf at the door and the Met Life merger having been scuttled the preceding year, John Carter convened a meeting of his senior managers in early 1990 to consider a proposal to sell all the investment subsidiaries— DLJ, Alliance, and possibly Equitable Real Estate and Equitable Capital—as a way of rebuilding the company's capital base. The investment subsidiaries, which had come to be thought of (by the directors) as Equitable's "crown jewels," had been the source of most of the profits in recent years. Equitable would be left with its "core competence"—insurance. At this meeting, Ray Colotti, a senior financial officer overlooking the investment subs, perhaps artlessly (but truthfully) observed, "But John, isn't that what Pan Am did? Sell off all their profitable hotels and other money-making properties to support a losing airline?" You could have heard a pin drop in the room. Carter was not amused by the analogy of Equitable to Pan American Airways, which had earlier collapsed into bankruptcy.

Privately I told Carter that selling DLJ and the other investment subsidiaries would be a big mistake—that the timing was all wrong, even if John wanted to do it later. At that moment, DLJ would have been sold at less than book value because of the depressed markets and gloom on Wall Street. Others might say that if I'd had any sense I would have agreed with John and formed a syndicate to buy back DLJ and Alliance at a deep discount. But I told him the truth—it would have been the wrong thing to do for Equitable. As much as demutualization itself, the profits from DLJ and Alliance later saved The Equitable from disaster.

When Carter's proposal to sell the "crown jewels" ultimately was presented to The Equitable directors, there was a revolution. Within 30 days a painful consensus developed that John Carter, a lovely human being who loved The Equitable, meant well but nevertheless had no solution to the problems. His latest proposal seemed one more step down the slippery slope of selling off good assets to avoid changing the old order.

On May 15, 1990, the Board asked me to become president and chief executive officer in addition to my role as chairman. Several directors suggested that Carter and I simply switch roles, with John becoming chairman and my becoming president and CEO. Remembering my experience at DLJ with divided authority, I politely declined. Old lines of authority die hard, and I knew the only possible way we could navigate out of the troubled waters was, first and most importantly, to have a strong CEO.

RX FOR A SICK MUTUAL LIFE INSURER

John Carter's sudden departure and my election to the chief executive officer role initially set off more alarm bells with the media, the credit-rating agencies, and, more importantly, with Equitable's field force of 8000 agents. The initial reaction was that the problems must be much worse than anyone had been prepared to admit. Fortunately, I had two things going for me: First, a past record of having resurrected DLJ from its dark days in the mid-1970s and therefore "being a survivor" in Wall Street parlance, and second, a good relationship with Equitable's field force. The fact that I had started my business career after college as a life insurance agent and that I had later earned a chartered life underwriter (CLU) designation upon coming to Equitable were in my favor. Equitable's investment subsidiaries also had performed well on my watch and this helped. The net of all this was that I had some time and credibility, both internally and externally, to try to turn the situation around.

Shortly after I became Equitable's CEO, the business and investment climate took a sharp turn for the worse. The Gulf War broke out after Saddam Hussein's seizure of Kuwait's oil riches. It seemed like history repeating for me—"déjà vu all over again," to quote Yogi Berra. When I had become CEO of DLJ in late-1973, another Mid-East crisis and Arab oil embargo had wrecked the capital markets and nearly put DLJ under (along with much of the securities industry). Here, in what seemed like history cruelly repeating itself, I found myself once again the new CEO of a floundering company facing the fallout from a global oil crisis.

The Gulf War happily proved short-lived, but more fundamental economic problems remained to haunt me for the next critical two years. The Fed's tight money policies, designed to curb the "excesses" of the late 1980s and thwart a return of inflation, continued to take their toll on the markets and the economy. Real estate values crumbled, bank loans went into default, the junk bond market (sans Drexel) remained comatose. Executive Life became the largest life insurance company failure in history. This was followed later by a more prestigious old-line mutual life insurer, Mutual Benefit, which was seized by the New Jersey Insurance Department. Its problem was too much illiquid real estate. The world's largest real estate company, Olympia & York, went into bankruptcy in 1992. The final casualty was President George Bush himself, who despite his Gulf War popularity, went down to defeat in late 1992 as the scapegoat for the weak economy (which by then actually was improving, but the public perception lagged reality, as so often is the case).

There were many times during the first two years after I became Equitable's CEO in 1990 that it looked—to the outside world and to some extent internally—like we might not make it either. With a financial institution like Equitable that takes in other people's money for safekeeping, confidence is everything. As the media, the credit-rating agencies, and, worst of all, our competitors began to target Equitable as a "troubled" company, our policyholders became increasingly nervous. We never experienced a "run on the bank," but sales declined and policy surrenders rose alarmingly, forcing us to hoard liquidity. We had to spend enormous amounts of time hand-holding and reassuring both agents and policyholders— as well as regulators, rating agencies, and the media—that the company was still sound and would survive this difficult patch.

Jerry de St. Paer, our chief financial officer, in a bit of gallows humor, quipped that it seemed like the company's name had been changed to "Troubled Equitable." Every story and headline seemed to start out that way. Over and over the media referred to Equitable's "soured" real estate investments and "junk" bonds (the adjective junk apparently being sufficiently pejorative not to require an additional gloomy modifier). I became painfully aware of a pronounced "piling on" syndrome in the media, as one bad story begat another. As a result of today's computerized information retrieval networks, no bad news goes unrepeated.

To counter the pervasive negativity, I knew I had to formulate a new strategy quickly, both internally and externally. I came up with a seemingly simple five-step program which I believed would turn around the deteriorating situation and get the company back on a growth track. These were (1) cut costs sharply, (2) strengthen management, (3) refocus on growth businesses, (4) install new incentives, and (5) raise new capital—the last step being the most important and also the most difficult because of Equitable's mutual structure. A sixth, unstated, goal I set for myself was "communicate, communicate, communicate." Our demoralized troops needed to know the truth of the situation, what we proposed to do about it, and where we were going.

First off, I knew we had to cut costs, in a much bigger way than had been done in the past. Because of the long-term, contractual nature of the life insurance business, there's not a lot you can do about past, unprofitable business that has been put on the books. If underwriting has been lax, you are stuck with it. You can't cancel the policies. The GIC losses were "baked in," literally, for years to come. But by reducing costs sharply we could reduce the hemorrhaging. I determined that I would cut operating costs by at least $100 million in my first 100 days as CEO. As it turned out, we actually ended up reducing annual operating expenses by $162 million, far exceeding my goal. Incidentally, I did *not* announce these cost-cutting goals until they had largely been put in place, with affected individuals told in advance. Nothing is more demoralizing for a company than to have the CEO, in a spate of macho chest pounding, announce massive cuts without saying who is affected. When that happens, everyone's morale goes into a tailspin.

I also knew that the easiest way to cut costs at The Equitable would be to eliminate some of the expensive, overlapping layers of management that had sprung up as a result of "downstreaming." Eliminating some senior executives also made the cuts at lower echelons more palatable. For example, Equitable had three chief financial officers (not including CFOs at each of the investment subsidiaries). There was a chief financial officer for a mythical holding company (perhaps "virtual" holding company would be a more modern description) that had been set up on paper—it was not a legal entity. This holding company and its staff watched over the "life company," which also had its own CEO, CFO, etc., even though it was the same legal entity as the holding company. Then there was yet another holding company, Equitable Investment Corporation, which also had its own chief financial officer (and staff) to watch over the various investment subsidiaries—DLJ, Alliance, Equitable Real Estate, etc. My solution was to go back to "one company." I was the sole chief executive officer and instead of three chief financial officers, each with his own staff, we had one. The cost savings from going back to being a single entity were enormous.

Other cost savings were designed to evoke a more Spartan mentality. These included certain largely cosmetic cost reductions such as the elimination of 13 limousines, no more fresh flowers daily in the office, a simpler (and leaner) dining room cuisine. (I had noticed a high percentage of Equitable executives and managers were overweight.) The executive dining room also went by the board; it had become gossipy and time-consuming as well as expensive.

Getting back to being "one company" also served to facilitate my second goal, which was to strengthen management. This really was somewhat of a euphemism for getting my own team in place, which I knew I had to do from my DLJ experience with divided loyalties. Because of our crisis situation, I did not have the luxury of a talent search externally, but I had been around Equitable long enough to form views as to who would get the job done. The departure of some senior executives and promotion of others unleashed new energies within the ranks of existing management.

There was one bonafide "strengthening of management" from the outside, however, and that was Joe Melone, whom I recruited from Prudential to be our new president and chief operating officer. Joe had been president of Pru, the United States' largest life insurance company and a triple-A credit at this time. Inducing him to leave and come to "troubled" Equitable was a major coup d'état and vote of confidence from an important industry leader. I needed someone with strong life insurance credentials to complement my Wall Street image (even though I don't believe I had ever been regarded as a "wolf from Wall Street"). Melone was widely respected in the life insurance industry, and his decision to come to Equitable was enormously uplifting to the morale of our troops in the field who began to brag that "The Equitable now has the best management team in the business" (since I had already been at Equitable 10 years, we can give Joe most of the credit for this rousing cheer of approval from the field).

My third goal was to define a new growth strategy for The Equitable—the "vision thing" that President Bush evidently failed to define in losing his reelection bid in 1992. Equitable had always seen itself as a "life insurance company." The agents liked to hear that Equitable wanted to be "the world's greatest life insurance company" because first-year commissions on life insurance were (and still are) higher than any other financial product. The only problem was that life insurance had become a no-growth business. First-year premiums for the entire industry had failed to increase for a number of years. As a percentage of America's income, I noted that life insurance had fallen from 5 percent of disposable personal income in the United States in the early post-World War II years to less than 2 percent in more recent years. The life insurance industry, once the premier provider of financial products for both savings and protection, had been left far behind by others, especially the mutual funds.

The decline in relative importance of the U.S. life insurance industry throughout the post-World War II period could be the subject of a much longer treatise. But part of it was beyond the industry's control. Americans were marrying later (if at all) and having fewer children. More women were working and becoming more self-sufficient financially. All of these factors reduced the need for the "protection" element in life insurance. Group life insurance, generously provided by most corporate employers, further reduced the market for individual life insurance protection. Cheap term insurance, with no cash value buildup, also grew in popularity, further eroding demand for the more profitable whole-life policy that had been the backbone of the industry's profitability. "Buy term and invest the rest" was a catchy slogan that further undid traditional life insurance.

But every sunset is followed by a sunrise, and it seemed to me that the new opportunities for Equitable (and its peers) lay in reorienting itself to the newly emerging market for retirement savings. I credit this view to Dick Hokenson, DLJ's demographically oriented economist, who drummed into my head the significance of our now rapidly aging population. (Strangely, although no one was talking about this in 1990, it's all we hear about lately.) As the enormous crop of World War II baby boomers entered their 50s the new risk faced by this group would be that of outliving their savings. Widespread cynicism among the boomers about Social Security was also likely to bring about a new interest in saving for retirement as opposed to their previously pronounced proclivity to spend.

At Equitable, I also noted that over half of our premium income was now coming from annuities, purely a savings product with some tax-deferred benefits, as opposed to life insurance. This had occurred despite almost no promotion of annuities as a product and despite the lower commission paid to agents on annuity sales. Moreover, the life insurance we were selling was now coming almost entirely from variable life, which allowed the policyholder to select from a variety of alternatives, including common stocks, to fund the cash value of the policy. While variable life provided life insurance protection, it also was an extraordinarily flexible savings and investment vehicle—in many ways superior to mutual funds because of the tax-deferred nature of the buildup of income and capital gains and the ability of the policyholder to shift from one funding alternative to another without incurring a

The three partners in 1968 in our new offices at 140 Broadway. From left to right: Bill Donaldson, me in bow tie and holding the then-obligatory slide rule, and Dan Lufkin. The notebooks to my left packaged DLJ's special research reports and were a trademark of our firm. Bottom, our prospectus in 1969, which shocked Wall Street, making us the first NYSE firm to go public.

PRELIMINARY PROSPECTUS DATED OCTOBER 7, 1969

PROSPECTUS

800,000 Shares

Donaldson, Lufkin & Jenrette, Inc.

Common Stock
(10 Cents Par Value)

All of the shares offered hereby are authorized and unissued shares being sold by the Company.

The Company is the first member corporation of the New York Stock Exchange to offer equity securities to the public. Although the New York Stock Exchange Constitution prohibits public participation in the ownership of member corporations, the Board of Governors has adopted in principle amendments which would, if approved by the membership, permit such participation (see "New York Stock Exchange Membership"). The possible commission rate changes referred to under "Statement of Income" herein, and other factors inherent in the nature of the Company's business, subject investment in the Common Stock to unusual and possibly substantial risk.

Prior to this offering, there has been no market for the Common Stock of the Company and no market for the common stock of any other member corporation of the New York Stock Exchange. The offering price has been determined by negotiation between the Company and the Underwriters.

THESE SECURITIES HAVE NOT BEEN APPROVED OR DISAPPROVED BY THE SECURITIES AND EXCHANGE COMMISSION NOR HAS THE COMMISSION PASSED UPON THE ACCURACY OR ADEQUACY OF THIS PROSPECTUS. ANY REPRESENTATION TO THE CONTRARY IS A CRIMINAL OFFENSE.

	Price to Public	Underwriting Discounts and Commissions (1)	Proceeds to Company (2)
Per Share			
Total			

(1) The Company has agreed to indemnify the several Underwriters against certain civil liabilities, including liabilities under the Securities Act of 1933, as amended.

(2) Before deducting expenses estimated at   payable by the Company.

At the request of the Company, 40,000 of the shares offered hereby have been reserved for sale by the Underwriters to certain employees of the Company and their immediate families. The number of shares available to the public will be reduced to the extent that such persons purchase the shares so reserved.

The shares of Common Stock are offered by the several Underwriters when, as and if delivered to and accepted by the Underwriters and subject to their right to reject orders in whole or in part. It is expected that the certificates for the shares will be ready for delivery on or about   , 1969.

The First Boston Corporation

The date of this Prospectus is   , 1969.

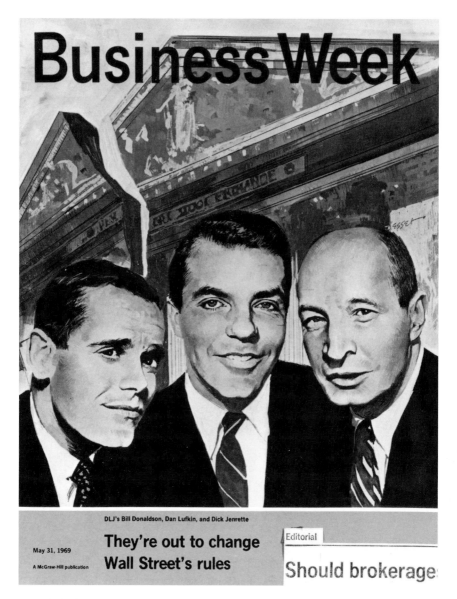

DLJ's bold decision to go public got us on the cover of Business Week *in 1969. The drawing showed the facade of the NYSE cracking while the editorial in the same issue endorsed our decision. Instead of cracking, the Exchange grew stronger with access to public capital.*

Some 10 years after selling the firm to Equitable, DLJ came full circle and once again went public in 1995. Shown on the floor of the Exchange, left to right: Bill Donaldson, recently retired as chairman of the NYSE; John Chalsty, President and CEO of DLJ, and also vice-chairman of the NYSE; Dick Grasso, chairman of the NYSE; myself as chairman of Equitable; and Pedro Galban, DLJ's investment banker on the transaction. Below, John Chalsty, my classmate from Harvard Business School, exhibit "A" of my admonition to hire someone smarter than you and they will make you look good.

We had a gala 25th anniversary party at Edgewater, my house on the Hudson, with over 400 friends, clients, and DLJ associates. The party, complete with fireworks, a train from Grand Central, and food and wine through the night was the ultimate example of DLJ's corporate objective: to have fun.

The press conference at which Claude Bebear, Chairman and CEO of the AXA Group, and I announced AXA's timely $1 billion investment in The Equitable. This gave us time to complete the lengthy demutualization process. Below, Joe Melone, president of Equitable, Bill Donaldson, coincidentally chairman of the NYSE, and I preside over the final step of Equitable's demutualization—a NYSE listing.

I was greatly honored to welcome the Emperor and Empress of Japan to my home in South Carolina as part of their visit to the United States in 1995. Shown above, left to right: myself, pointing out Fort Sumter, the Emperor, South Carolina Governor Carroll Campbell, the Empress, and First Lady Iris Campbell. Below, a chance encounter brought together the three founding partners of DLJ at a New York benefit in 1996.

Top, Equitable's spectacular
boardroom never failed to
dazzle visitors, including
Claude Bebear of AXA.
Below, surveying part of
the 30,000-square-foot
trading floor at DLJ's new
world headquarters at 277
Park Avenue, a far cry from
our one-room office 35
years ago.

My hobby out of the office is to collect and restore old houses. A sampling from my collection of six historic houses, clockwise from top: Millford Plantation, S.C., circa 1840; Roper House, Charleston, S.C., circa 1838; and Edgewater, upstate New York, circa 1820.

capital-gain tax. This was our answer to "buy term and invest the rest." For those not in need of life insurance protection, Equitable's variable annuity provided similar flexibility to the policyholder in choosing from among a range of investment management options. Giving a choice of funding vehicles to the policyholder—a creative idea pioneered by The Equitable—was a big step forward in revitalizing lagging sales of these products. Given the subsequent rise in the stock market, policyholders purchasing variable life and variable annuities have fared extremely well.

Unlike many of its competitors in the life insurance business, Equitable also had a far better developed and highly regarded asset management capability. Through Equitable's own investment subsidiaries and Alliance Capital (DLJ's former investment management arm), we had a first-class ability to compete with the best mutual fund managers as well as our peer life insurers. Alliance has long been one of the most successful pension managers in the United States.

Thus it seemed obvious to me that we had to refocus Equitable from being just a life insurance company, primarily selling protection, to being an asset gathering, asset management company. The big growth market staring us in the face was for savings, not protection. And we had a unique ability to combine the two functions—asset gathering and asset management—which would give us a competitive edge over most of our competitors, including the mutual funds. Our field force, which already was largely registered with the National Association of Securities Dealers (NASD) to sell securities-type products, gave us a big head start on our life insurance industry competitors. And our asset management strengths at Alliance allowed us to profit from managing the savings as well as the packaging and distribution of financial products.

With this new vision of a huge emerging market in retirement savings—through variable life, variable and fixed annuities, and mutual funds (through Alliance), Equitable was again positioned to become a growth company—not just a turnaround. As part of this repositioning, we later outsourced the disability income business and officially discontinued the

GIC business, setting up a huge reserve against future expected losses until the remaining GICs matured and could be paid off. John Carter had previously gotten the company out of health care.

My fourth goal was to install new incentives at Equitable which would create a more entrepreneurial environment, such as we had at DLJ and Alliance Capital. Since at that time we were still a mutual and could not issue stock options, we had to rely initially on cash incentive bonuses. Equitable's previous incentive plans capped bonuses at what seemed to me (from my Wall Street perspective) excessively low levels that did not really stimulate maximum performance. In removing these ceilings, we simultaneously capped all base salaries for a number of years. The goal was gradually to shift compensation more from the "entitlement mentality" of high fixed salary and annual raises to a more variable compensation structure, with bonuses totally variable with profitability and no upside limits. For the first time, we also extended incentive compensation throughout the entire organization, as some of the year-end payments that were routinely paid as an entitlement were shifted to overall bottom-line profitability. I believed these steps were essential to "bringing capitalism" to the "old mutual monolith" that John Carter had sought to change.

My fifth, and most important goal, was to raise more capital. Given the gloomy near-term outlook for profits, we somehow had to obtain massive amounts of new capital quickly. The credit-rating agencies were threatening to downgrade Equitable further, and the state regulatory authorities were ready to impose new, vastly more stringent capital requirements on the entire industry. I knew there would be only one answer—demutualization to gain access to the capital markets. But this was easier said than done.

DEMUTUALIZATION— THE WAY OF THE FUTURE

The cornerstone of my plan to rescue The Equitable was demutualization, a tongue-twisting term to describe the complicated process of converting a mutual life insurance company (owned by its policyholders) into a stockholder-owned company. The purpose, of course, was to gain access to the capital markets and allow us to raise much needed new capital. Having observed The Equitable at close range for a number of years, I had gradually come to the sad conclusion that no amount of cost cutting or even the most creative investing would be sufficient to put Humpty-Dumpty back on the wall. Confidence in the company as a mutual had been shattered. Outwardly, the company's ratio of capital and liabilities at 5 percent looked barely passable, but almost half of this was surplus relief (what I had dubbed a "headache remedy") that would have to be paid back out of future profits. Moreover, the erosion of the debt, equity, and especially the real estate market was such that we faced potentially huge asset write-downs on a $40 billion asset base which could have wiped out the company's remaining surplus.

The inescapable conclusion seemed to be that we *had* to obtain a massive capital infusion, and the *only* way to do this was to demutualize. At that point, the alternative of merging with another better-capitalized mutual had largely disappeared since (a) none of them were big enough or well-capitalized enough to take on The Equitable, (b) most of them were beginning to have their own problems with real estate and asset write-downs, and (c) by then, Equitable had begun to look "radioactive"—no one wanted to go near.

If the decision to demutualize seems obvious with hindsight, there were formidable obstacles that made many doubtful that demutualization would be our panacea. For starters, the New York State law allowing demutualization (passed in 1988, partly at Equitable's behest) had never been tested. Equitable would be pioneering new territory in what would become the world's largest demutualization affecting nearly 2.5 million policyholders. Second, the lengthy process of determining how much stock should be assigned to each policyholder in exchange for ownership rights was a knotty issue. Finally, everyone expected legal challenges given America's currently litigious state of mind. The head of Prudential predicted that it would take at least five years—"if it gets done in your lifetime!" Our own best estimate was two years, which we privately admitted was optimistic.

In listing the obstacles to demutualization, I should not gloss over the very real problem of selling this proposed solution internally. The mutual mentality was deeply ingrained in Equitable's field force, which for years had been extolling the presumed virtues of the mutuals vis-à-vis the stockholder-owned companies. I finally clinched that argument with a chart which I described as "the handwriting on the wall." It showed that 20 years earlier, mutuals accounted for two-thirds of the life insurance industry's capital, with stock companies accounting for only one-third. By 1990, the percentages were exactly reversed, stock companies were now two-thirds of industry capital. I cited this as evidence that stockholder ownership was the way of the future. I even had the temerity to call the mutual form archaic—and I still believe it is. Perhaps the most persuasive argument, however, was put forward by Harry Garber, Equitable's vice-chairman who had authored the 1988 New York State demutualization law. Harry told our agents that demutualization was a "win-win" situation for the policyholders. Not only would they get a stronger Equitable financially, better able to meet its contractual obligations, but also they would receive compensation in the form of stock ownership in the newly reorganized Equitable. That carried the day.

In actuality, the demutualization process took almost exactly two years to the day. It was a tribute to the hard work of Equitable people (demutualization, interestingly, galvanized a new work ethic at Equitable—people found they *liked* working long hours toward a stated goal).

But even if one subscribed to our two-year timetable for demutualization, the reality of the situation was that Equitable needed capital *now*, not two years later. My solution was to try to do a private placement of subordinated debt, which would be convertible into equity in the newly demutualized company once the process was completed. In effect we were looking for something that resembled a "bridge loan" to carry us over to the promised land of demutualization. Normally, raising a bridge loan of this sort would have been possible, even in the distressed environment in which we were operating.

There was one major obstacle, however, and that was the insistence of the New York State Insurance Department that they wanted a "market driven" solution to the thorny issue of determining how much equity would be given to the new shareholders vis-à-vis the policyholders. This sounds good in theory. In practice, how do you get an investor to put up $1 billion (the amount we finally determined was needed to shore up The Equitable) when you can't commit on what percentage ownership in the newly demutualized company the $1 billion loan would convert into? It was like asking the investor to play the equivalent of Russian roulette (something no fiduciary institution could do). Would $1 billion get you a 20 percent equity ownership in The Equitable, or 40 percent, or 60 percent? *Quien sabe?* had to be my unhelpful answer. Moreover, we couldn't even tell the prospective investors *when* they might get their equity since we didn't know how long the demutualization process would take, given the prospect of legal challenges, the new territory being pioneered, etc.

Our protests notwithstanding, the regulators were adamant, and so we set out, hat in hand, looking for our knight in shining white armor. The stipulations of the regulators—well-meaning no doubt—effectively limited us to large *strategic* investors, especially overseas investors seeking a stake in the U.S. life insurance industry, and wealthy individuals, not subject to fiduciary restraints. Under the rules that we had to play by, U.S. institutional investors, our natural market, simply could not commit to such a nebulous odyssey. Hank Greenberg of AIG offered $1 billion, but he wanted 100 percent of the equity in return. He was not about to get caught up in a game of Russian roulette.

In the end, we did find our white knight, willing to take a chance, in the personage of Claude Bébéar, an entrepreneurial and charismatic Frenchman who had put together The AXA Groupe, an agglomeration of French mutual insurance companies which controlled a publicly traded entity. AXA delivered $1 billion to The Equitable on July 18, 1991—just one day after Mutual Benefit was seized by the New Jersey regulators. If AXA's $1 billion had not arrived precisely at that moment, which we announced with great fanfare, the media's attention might next have turned to "Troubled Equitable." Instead, AXA's $1 billion vote of confidence turned the wolves away. We were off to the races.

To complete demutualization took one more year. We had to get the New York Insurance Department to approve the final plan of demutualization, which ran to 931 pages. Then we had to get a two-thirds vote, not easy in America, of voting policyholders to approve the plan of demutualization (we ultimately got 92 percent approval because all the bad press had so thoroughly frightened our policyholders that they eagerly embraced the plan). The final step of the demutualization process was an initial public offering (IPO) of stock, which under the terms of the plan of demutualization had to be at least $300 million of new equity. We ended up with $430 million thanks to our underwriters Goldman Sachs, DLJ, Salomon, J.P. Morgan, Paribas, and our own selling efforts. The final two-week, 28-city road show tested all of us as we were bombarded with questions about "soured real estate," junk bonds, the GIC problem, adequacy of reserves, and the usual litany of worries.

Joe Melone's sense of humor lightened the burden on the road show. At one point Goldman Sachs had us in two huge obscene limousines en route to another presentation. Joe had his limousine pull up beside mine, stuck his head out and said, "Please pass the Grey Poupon," a reference to a snobby television advertisement being run by the mustard purveyor at that time. Late in the day on another long, hot summer afternoon, Joe was told he was about to meet Udayan Ghose, one of the top analysts in the insurance industry. The pronunciation of Udayan's first name sounds like "you dying." Melone quipped, "You dying? *I'm* dying!"

What ultimately carried the day in helping us sell the deal was the redefinition of The Equitable, not as just one more life insurance company but as an asset gathering, asset management *growth* company. Our pitch—and it was true—was that the horrible GIC losses had masked some outstanding results in terms of the evolution of the new Equitable, which, with $150 billion assets under management at the time, had emerged as a premier player in the competition for retirement savings as the U.S. population underwent a major demographic change. It was like Cinderella going to the ball with a new gown. We demonstrated how Equitable's sales had shifted away from life insurance to annuities, a rapid growth business, and that assets under management—in mutual funds, pension funds, etc., at Alliance—were climbing rapidly. Our story was that, underneath all the asset write-downs and horrible financials, lay a sleeping giant, refreshed by the $1.4 billion capital infusion and now awakened to the possibility of being the nation's leader in asset gathering and asset management.

As to the GIC losses, we used AXA's capital infusion to set up $600 million in additional loss reserves to discontinue the business. Outstanding GICs had been paid down to $10 billion by the time of our IPO, and we promised no more would be issued.

Two years later the stock, which we had begged people to buy, had tripled in value. During this time, we also raised another $800 million for Equitable through the sale of convertible preferred stock, bringing total new equity capital raised to $2.25 billion. That's why I call demutualization the way of the future!

C H A P T E R

T W E L V E

EPILOGUE ON
THE EQUITABLE

Demutualization for The Equitable worked. As I write this, Equitable has now completed 18 consecutive quarters in which operating earnings improved over the prior year, resulting in pretax operating profits of $729 million in 1996. In 1995, my final year as CEO before retiring in early 1996, Equitable reported pretax operating profits of $574 million, versus $436 million in 1994 and $386 million in 1993, our first full year as a publicly owned company following demutualization in mid-1992.

During the three years following demutualization, we raised $2.2 billion of new equity capital for The Equitable which made possible another $900 million from long-term debt, well below the interest rates on the GICs that were being paid down. Including new capital raised for DLJ, which also was partially taken public in 1995 as part of our campaign to "unlock hidden value," and for Alliance, the other offshoot from my long-term management efforts, we raised a grand total of approximately $5 billion of new capital for the entire system as a result of the new access to the capital markets. Capitalism is a wonderful thing!

"Troubled Equitable" is again looking like a champion, and its earnings have been helpful in sustaining AXA's momentum. Total equity capital for The Equitable Companies now exceeds $4 billion, despite all the write-downs, with statutory capital of $3.6 billion in the life insurance subsidiaries. Equitable Life's ratio of capital to liabilities had risen to 12 percent at the end of 1996, nearly triple the level several years earlier.

Best of all surplus relief now accounts for only 6 percent of statutory capital. Meanwhile, the dreaded GICs, which once aggregated $15 billion in total, had been reduced to a paltry $291 million.

Joe Melone, whose decision to join Equitable proved prescient, became Equitable's chief executive officer upon my retirement, well-deserved recognition of his long years of industry leadership. In his absence, Prudential hasn't done so well—our gain was their loss. Claude Bébéar of AXA is now spending a week a month in New York as chairman. In the spirit of Equitable's founder Henry Hyde, who succeeded in his goal of becoming the world's largest insurer by the beginning of the twentieth century, Bébéar has a goal of becoming the world's largest insurer by the beginning of the twenty-first century. His recent acquisition of Union d'Assurances de Paris, France's largest insurance company, puts him close to this goal.

Equitable itself now has a market value in excess of $6 billion. Sweet revenge came in 1995–1996 when all the major credit-rating agencies saw fit to upgrade Equitable to double-A status during a period when many other insurers were downgraded. Sales of Equitable's popular line of annuities and variable life products are increasing at double-digit rates as the strategy of concentrating on retirement savings for aging baby boomers continues to bear fruit. Total assets under management in Equitable and its investment subsidiaries passed the $200 billion mark in early 1996. AXA's bold investment in Equitable has more than tripled in value.

CHAPTER

THIRTEEN

MORE LESSONS IN MANAGING UNDER ADVERSITY

The Equitable experience, which essentially was an exercise in crisis management, validated many of the lessons I had learned at DLJ and added a few new wrinkles to my evolving contrarian management philosophy.

As was the case in my DLJ experience, the single most important element, the sine qua non, of managing in a crisis situation is that there be a single, strong chief executive officer. When I became CEO of DLJ, in name, it took a year and a half before I was able to consolidate my authority. It's a wonder the patient didn't die while office politics raged, making everyone unhappy and draining our energies. I was determined that this not happen when I became CEO of Equitable. The situation was more desperate and the stakes far higher, involving millions of policyholders, than in the case of much smaller DLJ, serving only large institutional investors in the 1970s. But it was this experience with divided authority at DLJ that led me to decline the opportunity merely to trade titles with John Carter—he becoming nonexecutive chairman and I becoming president and CEO. What an invitation to feuding, fussing, and fighting that would have been! The dictates of courtesy alone would have hobbled me in dealing with the former CEO, whom I liked personally.

In any event, the emergency situation facing The Equitable led the board to back me totally. Knowing you have that kind of support is not license to become some sort of dictator or czar. But it did enable me to cut through the red tape, end the endless committees that took up so much time, and act decisively. It also allowed me to follow a contrarian way of thinking—that led to the contrarian decision to demutualize— to blossom. Everyone suddenly was encouraged to think creatively and challenge old ways of doing things.

Most importantly, the solid support of the board allowed me to implement another lesson from my DLJ experience— get your own team in place. You can't be a strong or effective CEO if the people below you are undercutting you or don't believe in what you are doing. Therefore, it is essential to get your own team in place—early on. In becoming CEO of The Equitable, I also faced a strong, immediate financial imperative to cut costs. This made it easier for me to clear out levels of redundancy in the senior management group. The fact that many senior executives were let go also made some of the cuts at lower echelons more palatable. This is a lesson many companies forget: pain has to be shared at all levels.

Getting your own team in place does not necessarily mean bringing in all new talent from the outside. At DLJ, because I knew the existing group so well, I largely promoted from within. Dave Williams was the sole exception; I recruited him to head Alliance Capital Management when Peter Vermilye, the head of Alliance, left following my decision not to sell Alliance but to keep it part of DLJ. That decision probably saved DLJ and maybe Equitable as well. In the late 1970s, Alliance was almost sold for $1 million cash plus a $5 million note. This compares with its present market value of more than $2.5 *billion.*

In the Equitable crisis situation, there was no time to embark on a search for new talent—with one exception—and I also had had five years to observe the in-house talent. The one exception was, of course, Joe Melone, whose prestige as president of Prudential and long years of experience in the life insurance industry was the perfect complement to my Wall Street/financial background. Melone, whose sunny Leo personality made him the perfect interface with Equitable's beleaguered sales force, freed me from 60 to 70 calls a day from worried agency managers, agents, and policyholders, allowing me to get on with the vital demutualization and capital-raising process.

Again, a word of warning from both my DLJ and Equitable experience, in getting your own team in place, don't clone yourself but rather try to surround yourself with people who have complementary experiences and talents. This means making sure you are well covered in all the key disciplines— marketing, finance, and manufacturing (or actuarial experience in the case of a life insurance company). You also need a blend of personality types that complement (again not with an *i*) your own skills—optimists, pessimists, traditionalists, contrarians, conceptual thinkers, and small-detail types.

I have learned over the years that small-details are not my long suit, but often are as important as the so-called big picture. More failures probably come from lack of attention to the small details of executing a plan than through lack of a brilliant strategy. I rarely seem to have the time or patience required to probe all the small details—and "the Devil is often in the details." Therefore, it is essential for me to surround myself with people that I trust who *are* good on details (which is not to say that detail-oriented people can't also be visionary). In Jerry de St. Paer, who became Equitable's chief financial officer, I found an individual with the unlimited patience and grasp of detail that made him the perfect coordinator of Equitable's vastly complicated two-year demutualization process. Similarly, in Bill McCaffrey, our chief administrative officer, I found an individual well versed in Equitable history (35 years on the job but still with a "young" attitude) and all the minutiae of how the company operated day to day. I felt I could sleep well with those two watching over all the myriad day-to-day details of keeping the company running. I decided that McCaffrey was Mother Equitable incarnated. Only in one case did I probably come close to cloning myself. Brian O'Neil, who became our chief investment officer, is temperamentally quite similar to me. But I needed someone to continue what I had been trying to do with The Equitable's portfolio: namely, resisting strong pressures from the credit-rating agencies, the regulatory authorities, and the media that would have led us to dump our real estate, junk bonds, and equities at what would have been precisely the wrong time, in the depressed markets of 1990–1992. Brian was also exceptionally articulate and reassuring in explaining Equitable's complex portfolio to worried agents, policyholders, and investors. He had an ability to make complex things seem simple.

The next bit of advice I would offer new CEOs (or anyone taking on a major new management responsibility) relates to the crucial importance of the first 100 days, or first few months, of a new administration. I am a great believer that every new CEO has a certain honeymoon period (perhaps 100 days) when people close ranks behind the new CEO, try to make the best of things, and are more amenable to change—if change is needed (and it usually is, if for no other reason than to mesh with the personality and working habits of the new CEO). People are also watching the new CEO much more closely in the early days for decisiveness and, above all, evidence of strong leadership and a sense of direction and purpose.

When I became CEO of DLJ some 21 years ago, I am afraid I badly flunked this test and totally missed my "honeymoon" period. I was stunned by how bad the environment had become in the capital markets (almost overnight) in the wake of the Arab oil crisis that hit just as I became CEO. Since I had been president and chief operating officer before Bill Donaldson left for Washington and turned the reins over to me, there really wasn't much I wanted to change at DLJ when I was elevated to the CEO role. I tended to react defensively when the storm hit, that things were OK—we just had to tough it out in a difficult period, which I thought was cyclical and would pass in time. This attitude made it appear that I was paralyzed—maybe I was! Somehow, miraculously, I survived this poor start. The point of the story, however, is that my inaction during the first few critical months of my new CEO-ship at DLJ made me look weak and defensive. It almost cost me my career.

I determined to act much more decisively when I became CEO of The Equitable, to take advantage of the honeymoon period to bring about sweeping change. I made this clear on my first week as CEO when I called all the key players into one room (one of the rare meetings I called) and announced my determination to reduce annual operating costs by at least $100 million in my first 100 days as CEO. Tell me how to do it? Within a matter of days, we found ways to cut $162 million out of annual expenses. This was a huge step toward returning to profitability. I also declared a moratorium on outside consultants (Equitable's outside consulting bills habitually were enormous). I suppose this could be considered contrarian in that so often new CEOs bring in consultants to tell them what is wrong. In this case, there was no need for further study. The real need was to act quickly and decisively to address the obvious problems.

From that first week on, I continued to take advantage of the honeymoon period to bring about sweeping changes at The Equitable, culminating in the decision to demutualize the company. As a result, by the end of my first 100 days, we had leaned the company down to fighting trim, established a new strategic direction for future growth (asset gathering for retirement), and developed a plan that would open the door to raising massive amounts of new capital through demutualization. The Japanese have an expression "Strike while the iron is red hot." This is good advice to new CEOs: Take advantage of your honeymoon period and show you are a leader.

C H A P T E R

F O U R T E E N

TURNING PROBLEMS INTO OPPORTUNITIES

The Equitable experience, above all, taught me the need to turn problems into opportunities. When I surveyed the situation upon becoming CEO of The Equitable, there seemed to be far more problems than opportunities. Business consultants (including my favorite mentor Peter Drucker) usually advise managers to "focus on opportunities, not problems." You really have to do both. The contrarian challenge for me was to find ways to *turn these problems to our advantage.*

The best example of turning a problem into an opportunity was the acute capital shortage which led me to propose demutualization. The contrarian decision to demutualize, going against the encrusted grain of an old-line mutual, was essential not only to The Equitable's survival but to its renaissance as a growth company. Even had there been no capital shortage, I am convinced demutualization would have been the right strategic move for The Equitable. The closed world of the old-line mutuals is gradually contracting as newcomers like Merrill Lynch, Fidelity, as well as up-and-coming stockholder-owned life companies like Sun America, and the banks, make heavy inroads. I can think of no really valid reason why a mutual life insurance company would want to deny itself access to the capital markets—short of the sometimes unpleasant task of explaining underperformance to shareholders. The charts I showed demonstrated conclusively that the mutuals were rapidly shrinking in importance vis-à-vis the

stock companies. I also felt Equitable would be better managed in the future in a public mode. The analysts keep you on
your toes despite complaints that they are too short-term oriented. There is no place to hide when you are public.

Despite the logic of the case, I seriously doubt that I would
have been able to persuade The Equitable board of directors
and especially our agents that we should demutualize had
there been no problems. It took a crisis to bring things to a
head. Even though I knew we had to demutualize to survive, it
was comforting to me to believe that we were doing the right
thing *strategically* for the long-term health of the company.
Today I believe Equitable has a big competitive advantage vis-
à-vis its traditional mutual competitors, such as New York
Life, Prudential, or Metropolitan in its access to the capital
markets. This is especially true today when companies must
redefine who and what is their competition. All the new competitors are shareholder-owned, with virtually unlimited
access to the capital markets.

Similarly, I am certain that had we not been confronted
with major problems, I could never have gotten a consensus to
cut costs as deeply as we needed to do. Equitable now does far
more business with a staff only slightly in excess of 4000,
down from more than 7200 when I became CEO.
Interestingly, with all the recent flap over corporate downsizing, I decided to look at total employment in The Equitable
family, including DLJ, Alliance, and the investment subsidiaries. I found that because of rapid growth in revenues and
profits at DLJ and Alliance, Equitable's total head count,
including the investment subsidiaries, now exceeds what it
was when I became CEO. Equitable has 12,500 employees
today (excluding agents) versus 11,500 in 1990. The new jobs
also are generally higher-paying.

We also managed to turn Equitable's bad press into an
opportunity of sorts. Every time a bad story came out in the
media, I used it to good effect in urging the regulatory authorities to speed the demutualization process. To their credit,
they did just that. We clearly were on a fast track at the New
York Insurance Department and later at the Securities and

Exchange Commission. I have already mentioned how the bad press undoubtedly helped us to get over what once seemed to me the formidable obstacle of obtaining a two-thirds yes vote from policyholders to approve our plan of demutualization. We got a resounding 92 percent yes vote.

While problems create an environment to bring about change, another important lesson I learned was *don't fight on too many fronts.* Once the process of change starts, it is easy to get carried away and make unnecessary or even detrimental changes and cuts. For example, many people urged me to take Draconian steps to cut our distribution costs in the field. Mel Gregory, a veteran Equitable hand whom I had brought to New York to head agency operations, convinced me this would be a tragic mistake. Mel argued that the agency managers and agents had already been subjected to so much harassment from competitors, policyholders, the media, and the credit-rating agencies that the last thing they needed was to become victims of more cuts imposed from the home office. I was rewarded by incredible loyalty from the field, which in turn was transmitted to our policyholders.

COMMITTEES, CONSULTANTS, AND CORE COMPETENCIES

As you may have gathered by now, a key tenet of my personal business philosophy, much of it derived from my Equitable experience, is to minimize the use of committees. Please allow me to ventilate a bit on the subject. I think they stifle creativity, waste enormous amounts of time, and diffuse personal responsibility and accountability. They also create jealousy: You may hate attending a committee meeting but, if they exist, you surely want to be a member out of self-defense to protect your turf. Rarely is the truth spoken at committees. In my experience they consist chiefly of verbal posturing, saying what the CEO (or person in power) wants to hear rather than the unvarnished truth.

Perhaps the worst aspect of committees is that they diffuse responsibility. If a *committee* has approved something, it is hard to pinpoint responsibility. Often they are used as a fig leaf to cover or give legitimacy to a decision the CEO or committee chairman has already made. Rarely are entire committees hung when decisions turn out badly. "Don't blame me, the *committee* approved it," is a defense hard to refute.

At DLJ we severely limited the number of committees, kept them as small as possible, and limited the number of meetings to the absolute minimum necessary for legal or other compliance purposes. As a result, no one felt left out. The few committees that did exist were not perceived to be important. No one believed that key life-and-death, go–no-go decisions were made in these committees. Dave Williams, incidentally, has continued this philosophy at Alliance, which runs lean with a minimum of committees and bureaucracy.

At Equitable, just the reverse was the case before I became CEO. There were committees for everything. Worst of all, the long committee meetings effectively wrecked the best working hours of the day. Under John Carter, as the crisis became more apparent, the corporate management committee, or CMC, began to meet more and more frequently and for longer periods. The meetings were debilitating instead of exhilarating and were accomplishing nothing other than creating more frustration and internal divisions. They did *not* bring the team together, one of the intended goals. To reverse this trend, when I became CEO I literally banned *all* preset, regular committee meetings. When we had to have a meeting for some reason, they were ad hoc and held after regular office hours, assuring a minimum of long-winded oratory.

My bias against committees does not extend to these ad hoc meetings, which were more or less spontaneously called gatherings of involved persons. Impromptu gatherings can often spark creativity. The very informality and temporary nature of an ad hoc committee mitigates against the posturing and ingrained rigidities that go hand in glove with established committees that meet on a regular basis. In contrast, I find that in established committees the participants already know their fellow members' biases, positions, and key beliefs. Members even gravitate to the same seats. There is no surprise, no spark, and the meetings become boring because the participants already know how the other members will react. The meetings clutter one's schedule and prevent spontaneous response to changing developments.

If impromptu, ad hoc gatherings—as opposed to set committees—are good, it is important that the office layout be conducive to such spontaneous "coming together" gatherings. The layout of The Equitable's offices violated all my rules for easy communication. Unfortunately, we were stuck with a layout that tended to isolate the senior executives in fiefdoms at each corner of the building. Ideally, executives should occupy relatively small offices (big offices for the senior officers are always a bad sign) in close proximity, preferably on the same floor as members of the professional staff. For some reason people seem to communicate better horizontally (even one floor is a great barrier to communicating). Secretaries or assistants should not serve as Praetorian guards, precluding informal spontaneous gatherings. This was a big problem at Equitable which I never resolved. Nothing is worse than to have a great idea bubbling in one's head and being told that you have to make an appointment, often on another day or week, to see a colleague. I also find meetings by appointment almost always last longer than needed. If you've blocked out 15 minutes or a half hour for someone, they inevitably will use it whether it's really needed or not. Many of these appointments, which clutter schedules, could be handled over the telephone or on the spur of the moment.

In that respect, I have always been skeptical of those executives who preplan every minute of their day. Not only does this deprive the executive of the opportunity to pursue new opportunities or great ideas that may appear unexpectedly, it denies one's colleagues access if every moment of the day is prescheduled. I am not arguing for total anarchy or a totally unrestricted schedule, just be prepared to change or alter it on short notice. Don't always force your fellow professionals to make an appointment to see you. There's no time like the present when an idea is pregnant. Strike while the iron is red hot! The contrarian manager hates to have every moment of one's life planned weeks, months, or years ahead. It's boring.

Much of the enthusiasm I encounter in those executives (or more frequently in management consultants) who are in love with committees is that they are supposed to be good communication vehicles. Most of the time they have the opposite effect. Those attending usually do not go back to their divisions, minions, or whatever and spread the gospel. Instead, the rank and file finds itself cut off from the knowledge of what has been decided. The CEO may *think* that downward communication occurs; all too often the message dies with the one who attends the meeting.

If committees are lousy communication vehicles, the reality is that one still has to find some way to communicate with the professional staff. This is especially true in crisis situations, when there is a high level of uncertainty among employees. I have always believed in erring on the side of maximum disclosure of key developments, policies, strategies, etc., to the professional staff, even though it will occasionally backfire. Morning meetings, weekly meetings, or whatever, at which every member of the professional staff is invited to attend can be useful. At Alliance Capital, portfolio managers and analysts meet briefly each morning as a way of sharing current research and developments. But these are not decision-making meetings. Intranets are the hot new way to communicate.

Because of my journalism background, I have always favored periodic written communications as a way to keep the professional staff current on developments, plans, goals, and objectives. Today this can be accomplished by electronic mail or closed-circuit television broadcasts of key events. A well-written house organ or newsletter or even a daily news bulletin board in a key location can be useful in spreading the news. The best communication vehicles I had at Equitable were periodic "Dear Equitable Associate" (not employee!) letters in which I explained what we were trying to do with the company and where we were headed. The candid, impromptu, and personal nature of these letters seemed to make them more effective than had they been printed up handsomely in our *Equitable Enterprise* house organ. I would just take pen in hand whenever the spirit moved me and let a message fly. The response was excellent. Ace Greenberg, whom I have always greatly admired for his spartan leadership at Bear Stearns, does the same thing to good effect, but he uses a mythical character called Haimchinkel Malintz Anaynikal to bolster his admonitions to be frugal. These memos were recently compiled into *Messages from the Chairman*, a primer for spartan management.

The best communications are, of course, tête-à-tête at an occasional dinner (in *vino veritas*), at social functions, bringing in spouses as well, and—above all—at fun occasions. DLJ has an annual Principals Dinner Dance and various other informal gatherings that facilitate "getting to know you" as well as communication. I like to open up my personal residences for company events and parties. People love to visit you in your home—it's so much more personal and says you care.

Communicate we must—but please, not in committees.

Aside from forming committees, synergy groups, or whatever, another much beloved nostrum of management consultants is the concept of "core competencies." Wall Street analysts are just about as bad in their disdain for things that don't seem core. The line of reasoning goes that if we can only figure out what the core competencies of the corporation are, we will know how to chart the future. "Stick to your core competencies" is the standard marching order issued by most consultants and analysts. The logic seems indisputable.

Yet the more I've seen or heard or thought about these so-called core competencies, the less impressed I am. Locking the company into its presumed core competence seems to me a prescription for corporate rigor mortis. The very idea that new competencies just might happen to develop within the company are given scant or no credence.

Under the core competence philosophy, you could put a pot of gold just outside the defined core competence of the company and it would be ignored. Not too long ago Dave Williams, chairman of Alliance Capital Management, and I sat in on a presentation by British management consultant (with a U.S. parent) to AXA, the large French insurer which helped rescue Equitable with its bold $1 billion investment "just in time." The presentation was all about core competencies in AXA and in Equitable. Inevitably, the core competence was defined as insurance. DLJ, in investment banking and securities, and Alliance, in asset management, were not classified by the consultant as core competencies. Dave Williams remarked to me that what they were talking about sounded more like "core incompetencies." Certainly some of the things Equitable had done over the years looked like core incompetencies.

The consultants intoned that AXA (and presumably Equitable also) had to define and stick to its core competence. Yet DLJ was earning something like a 30 percent return on equity and Alliance was earning 40 percent on equity. In contrast the core competencies in insurance—both in the United States and France—had, at the time, only very meager returns on equity in the range of 7 to 8 percent.

Moreover, the contribution of DLJ and Alliance was anything but marginal. At that point they accounted for over half of Equitable's earnings, which in turn were about half of AXA's earnings (even though Equitable is owned only 60 percent by AXA). It also seemed to me the consultants were ignoring the pot of gold (DLJ and Alliance) right under their nose. It seemed like déjà vu for me. Another prestigious consultant 20 years earlier had said that Alliance (money management) was not a core competence for DLJ, which was advised to stick to its then-troubled "core" securities business. Fortunately, we ignored that advice and kept Alliance. So far AXA and Equitable also have ignored the consultants' advice, as DLJ and Alliance have continued to grow and earn superior returns on equity.

The consultant addressing our group also failed to recognize change within the insurance industry. What we call the "life insurance business" in the United States today really has become more of an asset gathering, asset management business. Over 60 percent of Equitable's premiums come from annuities, primarily a savings and investment vehicle with very little to do with traditional insurance protection. Even the life insurance we were selling was backed by "separate accounts" invested largely in equities. "Protection" was a small element of the premium dollar.

The U.S. life insurance business today bears far more similarity to the mutual fund business than it does to traditional life insurance or the property and casualty lines of insurance. Yet the consultants sought to lump all under a core competence called insurance.

The reality is that financial services in the United States, once narrowly defined by industry lines, are all inexorably coming together. Merrill Lynch is both our customer and our competition. Ditto Fidelity. Charles Schwab is probably more of a competitor for Equitable today in competition for retirement savings than is New York Life. In this rapidly changing world, the narrowly defined concept of core competencies could be a prescription for corporate rigor mortis.

PART

THREE

GETTING
A RETURN
ON LIFE

D an Lufkin recently gave a speech on how to get a superior
return on your investments in which he concluded with
this line: "But we must remember that the whole point of all
this is to get a return on *life*." This struck a responsive chord
as I recalled DLJ's eighth objective "to have fun" and the DLJ
philosophy of keeping balance in your life. Dan's statement
embodies many of the things I want to say in this third "personal" part of my book.

Getting a return on life involves so many things—your
family and loved ones; your achievements at work or elsewhere; your physical condition and mental outlook; indeed,
your whole philosophy in life. That's a tall order for anyone to
even think about filling in the closing chapters of this book.
Instead, I'd like to pass on some of the personal disciplines,
ways of thinking, and philosophy of business and life which
have helped me to achieve more career and financial success
than I ever expected (if not in the *Forbes* 400 Richest
Americans category). Much more important, they have helped
me attain a life that has been happy and personally satisfying.
Some of these techniques may seem a little offbeat, but after
all, I'm a contrarian! They have helped me get a great return
on life.

HOW TO STAY IN CONTROL— OF YOURSELF

If you have a contrarian management philosophy, I suppose you are also entitled to a certain amount of contrarianism in your personal lifestyle. But regardless of whether you are traditional in your lifestyle or a contrarian, it is essential to maintain a certain amount of personal discipline in order to carry out your objectives.

First you have to define what are your objectives—business, personal, or otherwise? Just as a good portfolio manager needs to define a bogey—what is he or she trying to beat (the market?) or accomplish, so it is in life. Some of my more esoteric friends are into "visualization." They say visualize what you want to happen and it will happen. Recently I read that Scott Adams, author of the popular book *The Dilbert Principle,* has another word for achieving his goal: *affirm.* He affirmed that he wanted a best seller and he got it. Who knows? There may be some truth in his belief. I'm not one to debunk others' mystical faith if they think it works for them. It seems to me the best thing about visualization, or affirming, is that you have to decide what it is you want to happen. That's a helpful start.

But I have always had a simpler, less mystical way of managing my own life. I sit down every January 1 (maybe it's January 2 or 3 if New Year's eve has been arduous) and set down on paper my objectives for the coming year—the things I want to accomplish. I have two sets of objectives, one labeled *Business,* the other *Personal.* Usually I have 9 or 10 different objectives under each heading. Under Business I am usually quite specific. For starters, I put down what earnings level I expect our company to achieve in the coming year, and I also put down (solely for my own use) what I expect to earn in compensation (salary and bonus) if we achieve the earnings goal. Then I go on to list specific management actions which I expect to take during the year. At the beginning of 1995, my final year before retirement, one of the objectives I listed was "Take DLJ Public again," and, sure enough, we accomplished that in October. We also achieved the earnings goals and the compensation level that I had targeted. There may be something to this visualization!

I do the same thing for the personal goals, including repeating the compensation I want to achieve for the year and what I want my financial net worth to be by the end of the year. The other personal goals are usually less mercenary, including things I might want to do to help family and friends, or *pro bono publico* good deeds, or projects on my houses (I own six and there are always projects—landscaping, decorating, etc.). I always include some objective on my health, including a weight target that I want to achieve by year-end. One year my number one personal goal was to help a good friend, who almost died, regain his health. He has recovered, but I think the doctors deserve the credit. Even so, it was another win for goal setting!

I suppose there is nothing particularly unusual in this process, essentially the making of New Year's resolutions, which quite a few of us do. What I do differently from others is to coordinate this goal setting with keeping a personal diary (not a calendar, but a real, old-fashioned handwritten diary). This is my secret weapon and the way I chart my progress, or lack thereof, in achieving my goals and objectives.

I am a strong believer in the value of keeping a diary, not only as a means of keeping control of your life but as an actual management tool. Also it's fun (contrarians love fun), and the longer you do it, the more interesting the process becomes. *Like fine wine, diaries improve with age.*

I have been keeping a diary since I turned 40, so I now have 27 sets of diaries stacked neatly in my closet, handy for ready reference. I started my diary about the time DLJ first decided to go public, way back in 1969, when I had just turned age 40. I decided that "going public" would be an interesting process worth recording for posterity. Also I saw age 40 as somehow a midpoint in life, the passing over from the peak of one's physical (not mental) powers to the second half of life.

But I probably was really most motivated to do this by watching my mother keep her diary. She had started a diary when she turned 40. She was 76 at the time I turned 40, which meant she already had 36 years of diaries stacked up. (She lived to be 101 and kept a diary to age 95.) I used to go down to Florida to visit her in the small town in which she lived (Floral City, Florida) and there frankly wasn't much to do. To amuse ourselves in the evening, Mother and I used to pull out her old diaries, at random or for some specific event we wanted to recollect. It was fun reading her old diaries together to learn about times when I was a kid, or to look back at the entries during World War II when rationing affected everyone's life (just plain "life"—there were no "lifestyles" then as the nation was still coming out of the 1930s Depression and going into World War II). Evidently, there was nothing in her diaries that inhibited her from sharing them with me. I still have the diaries for the last 55 years of her life.

In any event, I was inspired by her example to start a diary on my own fortieth birthday. It's an understatement to say it has become an important part of my life and a useful management tool as well as a way to "stay in control of myself." The diaries are an integral part of my goal-setting process, which I go through at the beginning of each year. They also are my way of "keeping score" on myself.

If my first bit if advice is to set down your goals and objectives—business and personal—in writing, at the beginning of each year, then my second piece of advice is to *keep score on yourself.* The diary is an essential step in helping you keep score (as well as stay in control of yourself).

First, let me take a minute to tell you how I go about keeping my diary. Then you can probably find ways to improve on my method, such as doing it faster on a PC. I keep my diary in a small $5\frac{1}{2} \times 8\frac{1}{2}$ loose-leaf notebook. That way when I travel, which is frequently, I can always have some loose-leaf sheets handy in my briefcase, without lugging the whole thing along. There is then no excuse for not keeping up your diary when you are away from home. Some of the most interesting notes and observations in my diary often come while traveling.

Anyhow, the point is you've got to keep the diary current. Sometimes I miss a night or two—there are obviously some evenings in one's life when you don't want to be writing a diary at 2 a.m. But don't delay long. Write while the news or your thoughts are fresh in your mind. Actually, the nightly entries in my diary don't take more than 5 minutes, sometimes 10. Once in a blue moon I'll get wound up and pour my soul out to my diary for 20 or 30 minutes. But that's rare—usually only when something very significant is happening in my life.

I write my diary in longhand, in ink. But it strikes me that today's more modern diarist might want to type it on a PC. It would be faster and certainly more legible. There is, however, one important negative to this mechanized process. And that is the fact that my very handwriting itself serves as a sort of electrocardiogram of how I feel. When I am under severe stress or fatigued, my handwriting changes, becoming a hasty, almost childlike scrawl. When I am rested and "in control," so to speak, my handwriting is small, upright, and fairly neat (an assertion denied by my secretary Maria Fitzsimmons). Anyhow, I can detect major differences in my handwriting when I am very tired versus more benign moments. As I sit back and look at several days of diary entries, I can really tell when I need more rest or a vacation.

Some years ago President Ronald Reagan, on a visit to the New York Stock Exchange, remarked to me, "Tired people make bad decisions." At the time he was being needled by the media for taking catnaps in the afternoon. But it's good advice. Just by looking at my handwriting in the diary, I can tell when I need to take a break, slow down, or take a vacation. Doing your diary on a PC won't help in this department.

Look not for lurid sex details in my diary. There aren't any—at least not in my diary. Or hardly anywhere else these days at age 67! My diary is pretty much all business, which has been more or less my life story, though I do stop and try to have some fun along the way. I just don't think one's romantic life belongs in a diary. Some things are better trusted to memory. You have to assume the possibility that other eyes will see your diary. Indeed, most diarists probably harbor a secret desire that their diaries will be read by some caring soul someday. There may be a certain narcissism lurking in diary-keeping.

One other positive benefit I would accord to the nightly ritual of recording the day's events and your thoughts: it clears your brain and allows you to put the day at rest. Whatever is worrying you, write it down and thereby get it off your mind. You sleep better. In this respect, diary-keeping may have some of the same benefits some of my friends say they get from nightly meditation (something I've never been able to do for some reason). Another benefit is that you close the day with a feeling of accomplishment for having at least recorded your day for posterity or your own future reference.

But back to relating how I use this diary relative to my personal goal setting and keeping score. At midyear, over the long July 4 weekend (again assuming it hasn't been too raucous) I sit in the shade by my pool and reread and review the first six months of the year. As I read the diary, I make a monthly summary of key experiences and major events. This six-month summary then goes to the front of the diary to be reread at year-end before I begin the detailed reading and summary of the last six months of diary pages.

After making up my little summary, usually a dozen or so key events per month, I then review the business and personal goals that I had set for myself at the beginning of the year. These goals, by the way, are written on loose-leaf sheets kept right in the front of my diary, to be referred to easily as time passes. After I have reexamined my goals and objectives in light of the six-month summary, I assign myself an interim grade—A, B, C, D, F (sometimes I give myself Fs when I've made no progress toward a particular objective). If you didn't like the grades others gave you in school, this is your chance to grade yourself.

I know this may sound puerile to some cynics, but it works for me. If I've given myself bad midterm marks, I redouble my efforts to achieve my goals during the second half of the year. Also at midyear I sometimes will add or modify a goal, though surprisingly this is rare. I find I usually stick to the goals set at the beginning of the year.

This same process of rereading and summarizing the diary for the last six months of the year is repeated at the beginning of the New Year, preferably over the New Year's Day holiday. Then I give myself my final grade (in ink versus pencil at midyear) on each of my objectives. I've been grading myself for 27 years now—it's better than having someone else grade me. I take the process seriously.

Voila, that's it. And miraculously I almost always achieve my objectives or come close or at least have given it my best effort (for example, you can give yourself an A even if you miss an earnings target if the external environment changes significantly for the worse).

This careful review of the diary isn't just intended to grade myself—it's far more important in keeping control of yourself. As I reread the pages of the diary, I see ways in which I've been wasting my time. Or I see good ideas reappearing on which I have not acted, and so I wait no longer. You can detect from the diary when you're drifting or when you are really getting things accomplished. I find this review an invaluable tool in personal management and in helping me understand what is going on in my business. Sometimes it's even helpful in understanding the stock market. Routinely I note down any insights that might occur to me on investments. It's fun to check them out later.

Most of all, I find that the year-end process of reviewing the goals and objectives in my diary is something of a grand catharsis (like the nightly diary writing exorcises the day's care). I've put the year to rest. I've laid out my new goals and objectives for the coming year. It gives you a great feeling of accomplishment, and confidence that you are ready to sail into the new year with a compass to guide you.

So much for my diary as a key device for setting goals, scoring myself, and "staying in control of myself." But I have a few other tricks in this department which I'll pass on.

Perhaps most important is keeping accurate financial information on yourself. I have prepared detailed quarterly financial statements of my personal assets, liabilities, and net worth every quarter since I graduated from the Harvard Business School 40 years ago. I used to do it myself; now I have an accountant who prepares it. I don't try to mark my real estate, art, and antiques to market—they are carried at cost—but everything else—stocks, bonds are marked to market. I receive quarterly income statements as well as balance sheets on myself. I have daily access to the value of the marketable securities. The best testimonial I can say for this process is that I've always managed to make my net worth grow every year for the past 40 years (this is certainly tempting fate to say this—probably insures a decline in my net worth sometime soon). I mention it as part of the "visualization thing," or goal setting as I would call it. You must *plan* to grow in wealth. It doesn't just happen, at least not to most of us.

By the way, I don't pay much attention to comparisons with "the market." I've always felt money should give you peace of mind, as well as a financial return. I prefer to sleep well when it comes to my investments. More on this later.

If all this has not completely turned you off, let me suggest one final control mechanism that I have found useful. This one is a lot easier. Very simply, weigh yourself on the bathroom scale each morning before breakfast. There is, of course, nothing very novel about this, but I add a twist. I keep graph paper by my bed on which I plot my weight each day. (I also note events that might have led to an increase or decrease in weight. One recent morning I noted Bill Donaldson's 65th birthday dinner above my one-pound increase. Plotting these daily weights allows me to detect *trend* (remember the traders' motto *the trend is your friend*). In this case you must stop the trend if it is moving in the wrong direction. If my weight bounces up one day, I try to take immediate corrective action—no bread for lunch, no red meat, no evening cocktail. When I travel and can't weigh myself each morning I invariably gain a couple of pounds. But just seeing that upward blip on my chart when I return makes me take corrective action.

I now have 17 years of crumpled weight charts filed away. They show that, on average, I've gained no weight during this span when so many of my colleagues have inflated. I wish I could say this has led to a svelte waistline. It hasn't—some of it is redistributed in the wrong places as some of my friends remind me. But at least I have achieved stability despite all the business lunches and dinners, cocktails, wine, and personal repasts that go with being a businessman—or being retired, which can present even greater challenges to the waistline.

Aside from keeping weight graphs, I also do simple exercises each morning right before I shower—50 push-ups, 50 deep knee bends, running in place 350 times. I do this in lieu of going to a gym, which would probably be better, but I never seem to have time. Doing the exercise right after I weigh gives a certain urgency to the workout on those days when I discover my weight has gone up.

I remember years ago hearing Carl Hathaway, J. P. Morgan's head pension fund manager at the time, intoning that he never would invest in a company headed by a fat man (presumably a fat woman either). While one of my mottoes is "never say never," I tend to agree it's a bad sign. Something may be wrong. When I joined Equitable I could not keep from noticing an inordinate amount of obesity. I found it was contagious and soon I gained five pounds (later taken off). I even see it creeping into DLJ at times when people are under strain. As Martha Stewart might say, "It's not a good thing."

After reading all this "Organization Man" stuff (the title of a popular novel about the time I entered the business world 40 years ago), you may wonder how anyone so apparently disciplined can still claim to be a contrarian. The answer is that all these disciplines are simply the takeoff point for more creative thinking. Each of these processes—the goal setting, keeping score, the diary—all trigger alternative solutions in my mind as I review them. Take my word, "It's a good thing!"

THE SCARLETT O'HARA SCHOOL OF MANAGEMENT

As a kid growing up in North Carolina, I may have seen *Gone With the Wind* one too many times—or maybe a dozen too many times. Perhaps that's where I got my preservationist interest in restoring great antebellum mansions (or companies) to their former glory. But there were also some very useful management lessons to be learned from the story of Scarlett O'Hara, particularly how to survive under stress.

Scarlett's most memorable lines (as I recall them) were "I won't think about that now. I'll think about it tomorrow. If I think about it now, I'll go crazy. After all, tomorrow is another day!" Some might think this sounds suspiciously like mañana management, putting off what should be done today until tomorrow. Scarlett, however, could never be accused of walking away from a problem or putting her head in the sand. Her role model to us was to face life's problems squarely and realistically and do something about them, rather than simply wringing one's hands in despair.

I have found that there are many times, especially at night when one goes to bed under stress and can't sleep, when Scarlett's words can be helpful: "I won't think about that now. I'll think about it tomorrow." During my periods of peak adversity at DLJ in the mid-1970s and at Equitable in the early 1990s, I often recalled Scarlett's lines as I tossed and turned in my bed at night, worrying about seemingly intractable problems or demons that were pursuing the company and me. Scarlett's words almost became a mantra for me.

Nancy (Nikki) Green, senior vice president at Equitable and a great ally during the dark days at Equitable, used to call this Dick's "Scarlett O'Hara School of Management." "Tomorrow is another day" would certainly be the motto of this school of management. "Time heals all" (a favorite expression in the real estate business) is another useful tenet to remember as one grapples with today's problems.

Trying to get to sleep at 3 a.m. by simply telling yourself to worry about something tomorrow, rather than right then and there, is easier said than done, as most people have discovered. A favorite technique many people use is to keep a pad by their beds so they can put down in writing what they are worrying about so they can address the problem the next day. Sometimes this works and clears the worry out of your head (just as writing the events of the day in my diary right before bedtime seems to cleanse my brain).

Quite by accident, I discovered a helpful refinement to simply jotting down what was worrying me and keeping me awake at 3 or 4 a.m. And that was to *cumulate* and *retain all* the past lists of worries that I had noted on paper at night. Since I keep long yellow legal pads near my bed to jot down nightly worries (no wonder I never got married), there were several old lists of my nocturnal worries lying about. I decided it might be instructive to save them all, cumulate them, and later strike a line through the worry once the problem had been resolved.

What really amazed me about this process was that, sooner or later, I was able to solve *all* the problems that had seemed so life threatening (or more aptly, company threatening) at the time. This proved to be a great comfort to me on future sleepless nights. After noting down what was worrying me currently, I would flip back through the yellow sheets from prior nights. I would first look to see if there were any old problems listed that I could now draw a line through as having been resolved. What a joy to find I could cross out some past demon of a problem! And what a comfort to see so many lines drawn through past problems over the previous months. This process helped me put the current evening's set of worries in perspective. And usually this let me go back to sleep peacefully, recalling Ronald Reagan's line "Tired people make bad decisions," along with Scarlett's "I'll think about it tomorrow."

Ultimately, before Equitable's demutualization was complete, I found I had listed 96 problems (somewhere along the way I began to number them). I had been able to draw a line through every single one of them. I still save those somewhat frayed and battle-scarred sheets as a memento of a trying time that ended happily. It is a confidence-building experience to discover how many problems you have solved. I still keep yellow pads by my bed—even though I am officially retired—because there's always something new to worry about. I think I finally concluded that I *like* to worry. If there is no problem, I somehow manage to create one—always changing or rearranging things, always trying to improve things. It is a fine art to know when to leave well enough alone, an art I have not mastered.

There's more to the Scarlett O'Hara School of Management than simply "pack up your problems on an old yellow pad and smile, smile, smile" as they go away miraculously—though sometimes that happens. More annoying are the *daytime* problems that one faces, which often during Equitable's travails began for me in early morning when I opened up *The Wall Street Journal, The New York Times,* or some other publication, only to encounter yet another "Troubled Equitable" story about soured real estate or junk bonds (by the way, the incredible performance of those much-maligned junk bonds since the early 1990s warms my heart—the journalists, the rating agencies, and the regulators were wrong in so disparaging them). This almost daily sniping from the media, threatened downgrades from the credit-rating agencies, new delays from the regulators, or company bashing by competitors were all terribly demoralizing to my embattled troops at The Equitable.

To keep things moving, I recalled a quotation used by Albert Camus: "The dogs bark but the caravan moves on." In conversations and communications with Equitable people, I sought to portray these almost daily irritations as being akin to jackals snapping at the heels of the camels in the caravan. The important point is *not* to let the caravan stop and try to fight it out with the dogs. Rather one must keep the caravan moving. I reminded our people that we knew precisely where our caravan was going—to the promised land of demutualization with an oasis containing billions of dollars at which we could refuel and quench our thirst. We just had to keep the caravan moving and not slow down.

I found over and over when some new problem popped up that angered us, some one of us would say "The dogs bark but the caravan moves on." This would bring on laughter. We just ignored the snapping and yapping and kept moving on. And that's the way it is with life. Think of the President of the United States and all of the endless snapping and jackals barking at his heels every day. You can't stop and snap back or you risk being overwhelmed. Still more dogs will run out and start snapping if you stick around to argue. Just keep moving along!

And, of course, remember that as a good contrarian you're supposed to try to find a way to turn some of these daily problems into opportunities. Only then should you tarry. Since we are discussing turning problems into opportunities, I might also recall another thought-provoking passage from *Gone With the Wind*. Rhett Butler lets Scarlett in on a secret: "More great fortunes are made during bad times than good times." He was referring to the profits he made as a blockade runner during the Civil War. Rhett proved adept at turning the South's problems into opportunities, at least for himself.

Whatever techniques one uses to buy time when things look black or you are feeling low, I am always struck by *what a difference a day makes*. Problems that appear life threatening one day somehow seem to go away or recede in importance a day or two later. Why is it that some mornings we wake up with high energy and feel we can conquer the world, while other days we just drag along? Usually I find this has nothing to do with what transpired the night before. You can have high energy with little or no sleep. Is it body rhythms? Or does

astrology have something to do with it? I find I'm more ener-
getic when the moon is in Aries, my sun sign. I also seem to
have more energy at high tide (Dave Williams, my opposite
astrological sign Libra, says he feels more calm and collected
at low tide). Why are some people "morning people" and some
people "evening or night people?" I'm definitely the latter. I
get an energy burst about 5:30 p.m. each day when the office
gets quiet, just as others are fading. Knowing this I often go
on the offensive in late afternoon when the opposition is usually fading. Similarly, I resist breakfast meetings when I know
my energy level is low and my defenses are down.

I don't have answers to any of these phenomena, but what
they all say to me is that our bodies and minds are different
and constantly changing. If you're feeling low, take comfort
that "this too shall pass"—maybe through just the simple passage of time. On suicides, one wonders if the victim could
have only held out until the next day life might have looked
different and seemed worth living or the worries less threatening. Tomorrow is another day.

I do know that when you are feeling up, you should pour
on the coal and get rolling. Don't waste a minute when your
energy level is high. Think of all the things you've wanted to
do. Get on the telephone and start implementing. Get a lot of
balls in the air when you are feeling up. I remember when I
was being trained as a salesman at New England Life, my dis-
trict manager Reid Towler, a superb salesman, told me "Dick,
the best time to make a sale is when you've just made one.
Don't sit back and congratulate yourself. Go out and sell
someone else while your enthusiasm for the business is high."

We are all strange and different, which leads me to constant efforts to understand my friends, loved ones, coworkers,
clients, and adversaries—don't forget to analyze the opposition! Now let's move on to a few of my offbeat ways to try to
understand what makes each of us tick.

WHAT ABOUT ALL THIS ASTROLOGY STUFF?

The key to being a good manager (contrarian or otherwise) is understanding people. You may have brilliant insights, massive cerebral powers, or uncannily instinctive knowledge of what is right or wrong. But if you don't understand the people you are working with, their motivations, their prejudices, their essential natures—in short, how *they* see things—you will not get very far in implementing your plan. I remember being impressed with the title of a Broadway show years ago called "What Makes Sammy Run?" This may seem nosy on my part, but more often people are flattered when they think you are making a sincere effort to try to understand them.

For better or worse, I have gained something of a reputation for using astrology as part of this process of "Getting to Know You"—another popular Broadway musical ("The King and I") song. My friends kid me about it, but they—sort of— have become believers themselves. I must say it's surprising how many business executives can tell you what their "sign" is—there seem to be more "closet" astrologers out there than anyone is prepared to admit! It's certainly no weirder than Motorola having its executives sitting around in a circle beating drums in unison! Coolly intellectual Dave Williams at Alliance says he automatically now tries to find out someone's birthday when he interviews them. "Then," he says, "I call Dick."

I honestly don't know whether there is anything to "all of this astrology stuff" or whether it's just incredibly clever semantics that has somehow lasted thousands of years. But never mind. If it works in helping you or me understand people, let's leave no stone unturned. It's also rather amusing and harmless—why not have a few laughs along the way?

Indeed, I have used other such unorthodox tools on occasion to try to better understand people. Some of these techniques are a bit more fashionable with the scientific community. The use of handwriting analysis, for example, rarely seems to raise eyebrows. I have used handwriting analysis many times to try to better understand the people I am working with. My colleagues joke that they have all stopped sending me handwritten memos lest I subject them to handwriting analysis. Such analysis has been useful on occasion. For example, I was worried about a friend and had this individual's handwriting analyzed. The message came back, "This person is about to have a nervous breakdown." A few days later, that is exactly what happened! I knew the individual had been under stress, but I did not share this knowledge with the handwriting expert who made the prediction based on a handwritten note that I had recently received from my friend. This more than ever convinced me that there really might be some value to handwriting analysis. The more usual reason cited for using handwriting analysis before employing someone is that it is useful in detecting dishonesty. I wonder how the Barings's trader who lost $1.4 billion would have tested?

Handwriting analysis is more popular in Europe than America, made fashionable in part by the legendary late Sir Sigmund Warburg, founder of S.G. Warburg & Co. Sir Sigmund is said never to have hired a person without first resorting to a handwriting analysis, or so I have been told by his partners. I've often used handwriting analysis on important hires. When I hired Joe Melone away from Prudential to be president of Equitable, there was very little time to get acquainted because of the crisis environment. Joe, attempting to be discreet, sent me a handwritten letter after our first meeting. I never told him I had it analyzed, but he came through with flying colors. I've also used handwriting analysis on occasion when I simply could not understand the person I was dealing with. It helps.

Color chart tests can also be helpful in analyzing a person's nature. There is one simple test where you ask an individual, presumably a job candidate, to arrange cards with the eight primary colors in order of preference. Each color supposedly has a different meaning in terms of personality traits. The order in which you arrange the cards is supposed to reveal your true nature. I like to use it on friends at parties—just for laughs—the answers are amusing (usually). If, for example, you pick white as your first choice, it probably means you are indecisive. White is the color of indecision. If you are being tested for a job, don't pick black as your favorite color. It's supposed to indicate a negative personality. Black is the color of negativity. With all the world wearing black in recent years, there must have been a lot of negativity and hostility about. The person who first introduced me to this test confessed to having picked black and brown as his first two colors when he was tested as a job applicant. Black, of course, indicated he was being negative in his outlook (probably true) and his choice of brown as his number two favorite color was equally unhelpful in getting a job. Brown apparently indicates a love of luxury and comfort. This is probably why so many decorators use brown or beige in decorating—these colors seem to give a feeling of luxury and comfort. That may be okay at home, but it doesn't get you the job.

I will not give away the meaning of the other colors, but just for fun and to test the process, I once administered the color chart test to Bill Donaldson. But before I gave him the test, I noted down on a piece of paper how I felt he would rank the colors in order of preference (I thought I knew Bill very well). It turned out he ranked all eight colors in exactly the same order I had preselected for him. His ranking of the colors, by the way, indicated excellent business aptitude, unlike my other friend who unfortunately picked black and brown as his first two choices. Donaldson's top two colors were green and red [translated: entrepreneurial (green) and aggressive (red)].

Equitable, under my predecessor John Carter, also used an interesting personality test to understand the senior management team, based on having us answer several hundred questions. The test, which was called MBTI, was based on the work of Isabel Myers and Katherine Briggs (presumably the M and the B). At the end all of us were grouped according to our basic temperaments. I came out as an "Apollonian," which I thought sounded rather grand! The test showed that I reached decisions more on intuition and feeling, rather than on cognitive or judgmental thinking. I agreed with that assessment. What was so interesting to me was that everyone else on the Corporate Management Committee was so different from me. Most were "Promethians," described as follows: "They do not appreciate doing things that violate logic, reason, or principle or persons not using standard operating procedures." The test also showed I was more extroverted than others on the committee. All this confirmed my suspicion that I was a contrarian (if not an Apollonian), and clearly a fish very much out of water on that committee. I must admit that the test itself was fascinating. It did help me understand myself and to some extent, my colleagues.

Another new, allegedly scientific, study suggests that first-born children (in later life) tend to be more authoritarian and rigid as executives. "Later born" children are more likely to be creative and flexible as managers—or more apt to take a contrarian approach. As a self-styled contrarian, I was pleased to note that I was, in fact, the last born in my family.

Getting back to astrology, I never even knew what my sign was (it's Aries) until I was at least age 40— so by then I had survived half my life rather well without any knowledge of the subject. So can you. My introduction to astrology came in a rather unlikely setting—the swimming pool at the Pebble Beach (California) Golf Club. The occasion was DLJ's semi-annual Institutional Investor Client Conference. I had retreated to the pool, escaping one more time my friend Charley Ellis's efforts to indoctrinate us all with modern capital market theory (Charley's views on efficient markets, vindicated by the current popularity of index funds, usually fell on fallow soil, since to accept them would have rendered us all obsolete and possibly unemployed). Also at the poolside was June Rosenberg, wife of Barr Rosenberg, one of our brilliant guest lecturers on the subject of superscientific computerized and risk-adjusted asset management. June apparently had heard one too many of her husband's lectures and so was similarly playing hooky. I had only met June casually until this poolside encounter.

Astrology, whatever one thinks of it, is—if nothing else—a good conversation starter. It was in this case. June inquired my date of birth (April 5, 1929) and pronounced that I was an Aries—the first time I had known my astrological sun sign. Before the afternoon was over, June introduced me to further mysticism including auras, healings, etc., as she swept me in her car down the Pacific coast to visit the nearby Esalen Institute, something of a Mecca for New Age thinking at the time. Even I had heard of it. My most vivid memory of Esalen was of people exercising and jogging about in the nude (totally self-unconsciously) through the beautiful woods overlooking the Pacific. Sex did not seem to be part of the scene. Even so, it was quite an introduction for naive me into the uninhibited 1970s! At the end of the day, June promised to send me a tape from Maris Fletcher, her favorite astrologer, that would purport to explain my whole life history in astrological terms.

While I did not forget this rather unusual afternoon, I did forget June Rosenberg's promise to send me the tape. But, as promised, it arrived in the mail a few weeks later. I must say that this Maris Fletcher had got me down "cold turkey." Without ever having met me, she made so many accurate statements about my past life and what I was like that I became a neophyte-convert to astrology. To test Maris's astrology further, I ordered four or five other tapes from her for some of my friends. Their experience, when Maris's tapes arrived, was just like mine. They were stunned that she had so accurately described their past lives and key personality characteristics. We all ended up as sort of a Maris Fletcher fan club (only slightly tongue in cheek) from that moment on.

I regrettably never met Maris Fletcher in person, but talked to her over the telephone on quite a few occasions. She was a school teacher in Arkansas, a charming, kindly person all of us came to like and respect just through her voice on the telephone (or tape) and what she had to tell us. We used to swap "Maris stories" in our fan club. Alas, one day Maris announced to us that she was giving up astrology. I recall she said there was an illness in her family or some such reason, but she did tell me that some people (hopefully not me!) had gotten too dependent on her—would hardly cross the street without asking her if the signs were auspicious for such a venture. So Maris "retired." We were all devastated because she was fun to talk to and discuss people relationships. Her advice to me was unfailingly sound.

Too bad Maris withdrew from the field. With her Arkansas background, she could have been the perfect secret weapon for Bill and Hillary Clinton during some of their unnerving White House travails, rivaling Joan Quigley, the famous astrological advisor to Nancy Reagan. I must say her advice seemed to serve President Reagan well. Maybe that's why Maris "retired"—maybe she's the secret power behind Clinton's ascent from Arkansas to the presidency and reelection! Maris left me no forwarding address, and I hope she reads this to know that her fans remember her.

I never found anyone else (among professional astrologers) in Maris Fletcher's league. And so I began, in my spare time, to read and study some of the theory behind astrology. I decided to become my own astrologist. I learned, of course, that when someone says they are a Leo, for example, it only means the *sun* was in Leo at the moment they were born. It seems one has to check the position of all 12 planets, as well as the exact date, time, and place of birth to refine the process. As a result, all Aries, Leos, Scorpios, etc., are not alike.

In my case I discovered I not only had my sun in Aries, but a total of four planets in Aries at the time of my birth, making me a "true Aries." The only other Aries friend I have who beats me in that category is Dick Spangler, president of the University of North Carolina and one of the state's most successful business entrepreneurs prior to his academic tour. Dick has *six* signs in Aries, making him even more of an Aries than I. He's one of the few people I would not want to butt heads with. The sign of Aries is the ram, which likes to get his way by butting heads. I've been known to do that!

One key lesson I learned from astrology is that no one sign is intrinsically better than another, but they each are very different. Each sign has its strong points and weak points. An Aries like me, for example, must be the boss (or think we are). Aries, the beginning or first sign of the Zodiac, is supposed to be especially good at starting (beginning) new enterprises (such as DLJ). If we can't be the boss, we start our own company. Also, rams are stubborn—we fight fiercely and stubbornly when adversity comes (that trait helped in Equitable's hour of need and helped me hang on at DLJ when all was dark). We're also very truthful, sometimes too truthful for our own good, witness this book! But I also learned the Aries native has several key weaknesses, and knowing them helps me mitigate the effect. For example, Aries are notorious for starting too many things and not finishing them. Knowing this, I try (not always successfully) to avoid starting too many things, and I make sure that I finish them.

Because Aries are stubborn they don't know when to quit—sometimes one should just walk away. Like the ram, the symbol of Aries, we keep butting our heads against the wall. A Pisces (the last sign of the Zodiac) is supposed to be good at ending things and would be smart enough to know when to quit butting the wall. They dislike butting heads. Air signs like Libra or Aquarius, also disliking confrontation, would just float over the wall or simply walk around it. The other trait of an Aries that is both good and bad is that they are so spontaneous. As a result, Aries is rarely indecisive—unlike Gemini natives who typically seem to have trouble making up their minds. All my Gemini friends, such as Bill Donaldson or Charlie Duell, a close ally in preservation, like to play Hamlet—"to be or not to be." An Aries partner can help a Gemini partner be more decisive. Similarly, the Gemini can slow down the Aries' express, which is prone to act too quickly. Bill Donaldson's favorite expression whenever I proposed something was "Let's sleep on it." Mine to him was "Let's get on with it!" We have remained good friends despite our differing temperaments—astrology helps me (and can help you) understand and appreciate the differences in how each of us responds to events.

I've used Aries as an example of the good and bad in each sign, but a few more examples relating to other signs may be illustrative of how astrology helps me try to understand people. Leos usually are the best looking and most gregarious of all the signs. Things come easy for them. Bill Clinton, a Leo, can be so charming that, I suspect, all his life he's been able to talk his way out of any tough spot. This faculty sometimes leads Leos to take shortcuts, or "wing it." Leos (unlike Aries) also have a hard time tolerating very strong personalities around them—the Leo lion likes to be undisputed king of the jungle. It's a bit surprising that Al Gore, a strong Aries, has (apparently) gotten along so well with our Leo president. But Leos *are* magnificent—give them their due. Claude Bébéar, my white knight at AXA, is a classic Leo. Everything he does is first-class, typical of Leos. He walks into a room and things come alive, people feel better somehow. Nothing seems to get him down (President Clinton is similarly upbeat in the face of adversity.) Like the sun, their sign, Leos radiate sunshine. Joe Melone, who succeeded me as CEO of Equitable, also is a sunny Leo. It's impossible to feel angry around him.

Not so for the hard-working, determined wintry Capricorn whose dedication to work can sometimes lead to a grim, skeptical view of the world. They plan everything far in advance, down to every last detail. They hate surprises. Capricorns tend to be skeptical, in contrast to Leo optimism. They often seem old beyond their years. I personally like having Capricorns around because they are so good at details (which bore me). John Castle at DLJ and Jerry de St. Paer at Equitable, both Capricorns, were essential to me in implementing my schemes. But they will only serve you so long—you have to get out of their way sooner or later and let them keep climbing to the top. The mountain goat, sign of a Capricorn, has to keep climbing to the top of the mountain, patiently, ploddingly. Richard Nixon is a perfect example of a Capricorn finally getting to the top. Even after they get knocked down, they climb back up the ladder. They get there by hard work and time in grade. Usually they are not contrarians. They achieve their goals the tried and true way and have things planned down to the last detail.

What possible business application can all this astrological chitchat have? If I have not lost you by now, bear on. In prior chapters I have mentioned on several occasions the importance of *not* cloning yourself in forming your management team. When everyone thinks alike ("group think"), you're heading for trouble. Yet there seems to be some centrifugal force or narcissistic impulse that impels each of us, as managers, to do precisely that—surround ourselves with people who think and act as we do. That may be comfortable, but it gives an unbalanced view of the world. Bob Kenmore told me this story about Kenton, a company he cofounded that went broke after buying Cartier, the jeweler, and going on a massive expansion binge some years ago. Bob told me that he and his cofounder Gardiner Dutton, another HBS Baker Scholar, suddenly figured out that all five members of their executive committee were Aries, including the two of them. Aries often act too quickly and impulsively if not restrained by other more cautious signs. Kenton's five Aries were all too much alike in temperament and overexpanded badly. Sorry, Mae West. Too much of a good thing is not *always* wonderful.

When Equitable first acquired DLJ, John Castle—who had not been keen on the transaction but by then had become somewhat intrigued by astrology—made this interesting observation to me: "Equitable is a Virgo company" (this from an MIT graduate!). He was right. Coy Eklund, the former CEO and a director was a Virgo; John Carter, his successor as CEO was a Virgo; Leo Walsh, chief investment officer and soon-to-be chief operating officer was a Virgo; Bob Hendrickson, vice chairman and once a candidate to be CEO, was a Virgo. On Equitable's board of directors we counted no less than seven Virgos, or roughly a third of the board versus a statistical probability of 1 in 12. John Castle was right. At its core, Equitable had become a "Virgo" company.

Now there's nothing wrong with Virgos per se—I love them. They are certainly hardworking—no playboys they. But so many together? Virgo's astrological motto is "I serve." Not surprisingly, Equitable was one of the most "do good" companies imaginable. There was rarely a good cause that did not win Equitable's financial support, despite the company's waning fortunes. Virgos, I have found, are the world's best critics. But when you get so many together, they end up choosing sides and criticizing one another. I've found Virgos are at their best as analysts and critics, where they excel, but preferably not the head of the company. Their critical faculties make them excellent investors. Warren Buffett, a Virgo, is the most brilliant analyst and investor I know, but was less successful when he stepped in to try to right Salomon Brothers, after its problems with the federal government threatened to destroy the firm. He had the good sense to step back once the crisis was past. Buffett wisely keeps his own organization very small. Dan Lufkin, my Virgo partner, never liked large organizations and has been most successful and happy as an investor rather than trying to manage a large organization.

Two Virgos that have been eminently successful as heads of Wall Street firms are Ace Greenberg (Bear Stearns) and Phil Purcell (Dean Witter). Both seemed to succeed by frugality and simplification. Now Purcell is about to become chief executive officer of the combined Morgan Stanley Dean Witter Discover, arguably one of the world's most complex companies as well as the largest securities firm. Purcell is fortunate to have John Mack, a Scorpio, as his next in command. If any sign can cope with complexity it's Scorpio—they thrive on it! Purcell, however, will have to be careful of the Virgo tendency to nitpicking criticism. Scorpios usually don't take too kindly to criticism.

I personally like having Virgos around me because they don't hesitate to tell me how stupid some of my ideas are (remember, Virgos are the world's best critics—they hit the mark with deadly accuracy). Aries tends to have a strong enough ego to withstand and even appreciate Virgo's trenchant criticisms. Virgo, in turn, would be well advised to stick with those signs, like Aries or Leo, that can survive or even appreciate their criticisms. Dorothy Parker's lethal wit was quintessential Virgo.

Another sign that intensely dislikes criticism (such as Virgos habitually dish out) is Libra. Libra is an "air sign" whose motto is "balance." They make good judges, impartially weighing all sides. After they have very carefully weighed all sides before making a decision, their innate response to criticism is "How can you possibly question me?" If you keep criticizing Libras, they will simply fly away—like good air signs—and find work elsewhere.

My key Libra ally over the years has been Dave Williams, who has done an absolutely brilliant job of building Alliance Capital from $7 billion to $183 billion assets under management in the 20 years we've been partners. Long ago I decided he was so good I would never criticize him, and so we get along famously. I may ask a question sometimes or quietly slip little notes with my pet ideas. But to shout, "You're wrong Dave!" No way. That would end a beautiful, successful relationship. Libras hate conflict (I sometimes think Aries like it).

Dave Williams was born on October 5 (Libra) and I was born on April 5 (Aries). On the Zodiac, our two birthday signs are exactly 180 degrees opposite, six months apart. Aries is a hot, impetuous fire sign. Libra is a cool, detached air sign. Libras like calm. The difference in the two personalities is perhaps well illustrated by this story: Dave Williams and I were sitting by the river at Edgewater, my house up the Hudson. The river is still quite tidal that far inland. It was low tide as we sat there, the water had receded far out and was serene and dead calm. Dave, revealing his Libra love for calm, remarked that he always liked low tide, when the water was so far out, so calm, so peaceful. I suddenly realized I (as an Aries) was just the opposite. I've always preferred high tide at Edgewater, with the waves lapping against my sea wall, generating a feeling of excitement and energy.

Does that mean Dave and I are incompatible? Not at all. If we understand and respect our differences, we can help one another. One or the other of us will always be "in synch," so to speak. The two signs complement each other *if* each recognizes the other's strengths and weaknesses.

I could go on with lots of other hints that might help you succeed (by astrology) in business—or romance—and can't resist a few more one-liners.

Leos love praise (their weakness). Tell them how wonderful they are—conveniently, they usually are—and you will get along famously with your Leo. Virgo, on the other hand, is deeply suspicious of anything that smacks of flattery. Being practically martyrs, they accept criticism, perhaps too willingly for their own good, and adapt. Scorpios are another sign that you should not criticize. I have found they are usually so capable they don't need criticism. John Chalsty, CEO of DLJ, born on November 7, personifies the powerful and capable Scorpio executive. Never cross them; they can sting if provoked. Just act hurt—that gets to them. Praise works far better in motivating Scorpios, though that is probably universally true for *all* people. I hope this advice will help Phil Purcell in working with Scorpio John Mack in their new "marriage of equals," as it's billed.

Interested in politics? Find yourself an Aquarius—they are the world's best politicians—including Franklin D. Roosevelt (four terms!), Ronald Reagan, Abraham Lincoln, George Washington (born on the cusp). Aquarians have been elected president of the United States in 1 out of 5 elections versus a statistical probability of 1 in 12. No wonder we celebrate Presidents' Day in mid-February (during Aquarius). Their secret? They feel they belong to the people (the Age of Aquarius), and they sense what the people want to hear (and don't hesitate to say it). Keep an eye on Aquarian Dick Gephardt, minority leader of the Democrats in Congress. He could be a serious challenger to Aries Al Gore, the frontrunner to succeed Bill Clinton as President. Aquarians seem more drawn to running the nation than individual companies, judging by the seeming paucity of Aquarian CEOs vis-à-vis their stunning success in getting elected President.

I'm going to stop here because I think by now I've offended almost everyone. By the way, if an Aries gets mad and criticizes you, just act hurt and wait. It won't be long before the Aries comes back, tail curled under, and apologizes for being so mean. The Aries, if angered, tends to get it out of his or her system (Claude Bébéar says I "erupt like a volcano" periodically—he's right). At the other extreme, Scorpios and Capricorns tend to bottle up and conceal their anger. You unfortunately may never realize when you've deeply offended them but *they* never forget. For mental health, I've always thought it was better to ventilate and get what is bugging you out in the open. But sometimes this leaves permanent wounds.

The point of all this is that we are what we are. I can't keep from erupting sometimes when I'm offended. But I think my knowledge of astrology, even if it is all hocus-pocus and just imagined, is helpful to me because it forces me to think about what others are like, what is their essential nature. Aries, at worst, can be self-centered. Thinking about what the other person is like, is capable of, and is thinking, helps me be a better manager. Astrology has also helped me understand myself better.

The bottom line is that no one sign is inherently good or bad or better than another. I've never felt Pisces, the most changeable sign, were the best leaders of companies, because of their frequent flip-flops. But look at Michael Eisner at Disney and Sandy Weill at Travelers—both highly successful Pisces CEOs. They do change their minds quickly (witness, Michael Ovitz, the short-lived president of Disney). Pisces typically are best at *ending* things, usually situations that need ending (Gorbachev, a Pisces who ended the Soviet Union, is a classic example as is deKlerk, who ended apartheid in South Africa). I also read in *Forbes* that there are more Pisces billionaires than any other sign. Their instincts, insights, and especially their innate ability to sense when it's time to get out make them rich. Larry Tisch, a Pisces, is exhibit A in that category. Sandy Weill also seems to sense when something is ending and knows when to sweep in for a bargain purchase. Virgos, whom I've similarly despaired in the CEO role, also make fabulous investors because they are such keen observers, analysts, and critics. Warren Buffett and Dan Lufkin epitomize this.

I haven't talked about Sagittarians or Taureans—they are a lot like Aries. They like being their own boss, hate meetings as a waste of time, and work quickly and furiously to get things done. They just "go ahead and do it." Maria Fitzsimmons, my Sagittarian secretary, and Taurean Dick Pechter, who used to be my CFO at DLJ and now runs all of DLJ's retail and correspondent securities business, are wonderful for me to work with. They suit my personality. They just go ahead and get things done without a lot of fuss, fanfare, meetings, or complaints.

I also have not mentioned Cancer, a sign that often confuses me because—like their symbol, the crab—they have an outer protective shell to protect their inner vulnerability. They can be crabby—witness Bob Baldwin who shook up Morgan Stanley and Wall Street with his blunt advice. Dick Fisher, Baldwin's successor as CEO of Morgan Stanley, is also a Cancer, but his Leo moon gives him a sunnier personality. Cancers are real homebodies—their workplace needs to be like home. Don Marron, PaineWebber's Cancer CEO, keeps favorite artworks in his office to make it seem more like home. Bill McCaffrey, Equitable's chief operating officer, also epitomizes this trait—he just loves his place of work and his home and doesn't like to travel. He's been at Equitable for 40 years. Cancers would rather be at home than anywhere else.

So much for all these generalities. Most of the daily and monthly bits of astrological advice that you see in the media should not be taken too seriously. You certainly should not let astrology run your life, as Maris Fletcher feared was the case with some of her clients. Yet even if you don't believe astrology, it still can be helpful in forcing you to think what a person is like. And, as I found out with June Rosenberg, it's a good conversation starter (though some people will think you are crazy). How many times I've been trapped at a dull dinner party with nothing to say to the person seated on either side. If all else fails, try steering the conversation to astrology. It's surprising how often a lively discussion will spring up. The table that follows will help you find your sun sign and get started.

Final message—take all this with a grain of salt. I do!

Use this chart to find your astrological sun sign. Remember that all Leos, Aries, etc. are not the same. You need to look at the position of all the other planets at the time of your birth for a more complete picture. This means buying somebody else's book.

Astrological Sun Signs

ORDER	SIGN	NATURE	DATE	SOME EXAMPLES PAST AND PRESENT
First	Aries	Fire	March 21–April 20	John Whitehead (Goldman Sachs), C. D. Spangler, Jr., Dick Jenrette (DLJ/Equitable), Brooke Astor, Al Gore, Steve Spurrier, J. P. Morgan, Andrew Mellon
Second	Taurus	Earth	April 21–May 21	Hank Greenberg (AIG), Bob Linton (Drexel), Harry Truman
Third	Gemini	Air	May 22–June 21	Bill Donaldson (DLJ/NYSE), Joe Roby (DLJ), Hugh McColl (NationsBank), John F. Kennedy, George Bush
Fourth	Cancer	Water	June 22–July 23	Joe Dionne (McGraw-Hill), Steve Forbes, Don Marron (Paine Webber), Julian Robertson (Tiger), Bob Baldwin (Morgan Stanley), Dick Fisher (Morgan Stanley)
Fifth	Leo	Fire	July 24–Aug. 23	George Soros, Claude Bébéar (AXA), Joe Melone (Equitable), Martha Stewart, Bill Clinton
Sixth	Virgo	Earth	Aug. 24–Sept. 23	Warren Buffett, Ace Greenberg (Bear Stearns), Phil Purcell (Dean Witter), Jay Pritzker, Dan Lufkin (DLJ), Paul Volcker, Robert Rubin
Seventh	Libra	Air	Sept. 24–Oct. 23	Dave Williams (Alliance), Dwight D. Eisenhower, Jimmy Carter
Eighth	Scorpio	Water	Oct. 24–Nov. 22	Jack Welch (General Electric), Bill Gates (Microsoft), John Chalsty (DLJ), John Mack (Morgan Stanley), Hillary Clinton
Ninth	Sagittarius	Fire	Nov. 23–Dec. 21	Mike Milken (Drexel), John Gutfreund (Salomon), Don Regan (Merrill Lynch)

Astrological Sun Signs (*Continued*)

Order	Sign	Nature	Date	Some Examples Past and Present
Tenth	Capricorn	Earth	Dec. 22–Jan. 20	John Weinberg (Goldman Sachs), Bill Schreyer (Merrill Lynch), Dan Tully (Merrill Lynch), John Castle (Castle Harlan), Jon Corzine (Goldman Sachs), Richard Nixon
Eleventh	Aquarius	Air	Jan. 21–Feb. 19	Arthur Levitt (SEC), Abraham Lincoln, Ronald Reagan, Franklin D. Roosevelt, Dick Gephardt
Twelfth	Pisces	Water	Feb. 20–March 20	Larry Tisch (Loews), Sandy Weill (Travelers), Michael Eisner (Disney), Lew Gerstner (IBM), Alan Greenspan

THE DEMISE OF CONTRARIAN INVESTING

After a chapter on astrology, perhaps I had better get back on terra firma where my credentials are better established. Most of my friends who heard I was writing a book about contrarian management automatically assumed I was writing about contrarian *investing*. Since I have been responsible for managing other people's money (O.P.M. as we say on Wall Street) for nearly 40 years, I would be remiss if I did not pass on some contrarian thoughts as they pertain to money management.

My career in investment management began shortly after graduation from the Harvard Business School. I will tell you a bit about what it was like to manage money 40 years ago because times have so changed. The contrast is startling. Brown Brothers Harriman & Co. started me with the messengers, lugging bags of securities from firm to firm (would today's ambitious Harvard Business School graduates tolerate that?). Deliveries were made to something called *the cage*, which looked like its name. This traditional rite of starting as a messenger was evidently intended to bring young dandies down to earth while also letting them find their way around Wall Street. I was also told it would look good in my obituary..."He started on Wall Street as a messenger and rose to...." Next I was rotated throughout all departments of the bank, including a year or so tour of duty as an analyst in the research department. Great stress was put on precise writing skills in communicating recommendations. This certainly helped me in later years in editing DLJ research reports, especially the fine Wall Street art of hedging recommendations. I learned all about topic sentences (each paragraph had to begin with one), as well as market corrections, from Bud Newquist, the head of Brown Brothers research. Then I was assigned, more or less indefinitely, to the Investment Advisory Department as a portfolio manager for large individual client portfolios. Brown Brothers seemed to specialize in managing old family money, generally friends of partners. In those days we were closely supervised, working from an approved list and more or less plugging in stocks (or bonds) to fit the risk profile or income needs of the individual clients. Income, cash dividends and interest, was very important as one was never, ever supposed to invade principal. I always thought that the term *invading principal* was a marvelous choice because it sounds profligate, as intended. This was long before total-return investing became fashionable.

By today's go-go standards Brown Brothers's modus operandi seemed quaint. We wrote letters to clients whenever we wanted to make a change in the portfolio, citing a few reasons why and requesting them to sign and return a copy of the letter as our authorization to proceed with the transaction. This could take a week or 10 days ("snail mail" in today's vernacular). Only then could the recommended purchases or sales be implemented. It's hard to imagine today's young gunslinger portfolio managers operating in such a slow-moving environment. But there was a reason for the letters of authorization. Memories of stock market crises during the Depression were still vivid, and discretionary management of other people's money was viewed as fraught with peril for the investment adviser. It was much safer to get the client's written consent. Everything proceeded at a leisurely pace. It seems ironic that in today's far more litigious environment these concerns have been dismissed, in the absence of a severe market correction in so many years.

All these letters to clients were edited by the department head before being sent. Perhaps senior managers were not required to submit to this review, but the "younger fry," as we were called, had our letters closely monitored before mailing. One criticism I received still stands out in my mind. I composed a letter to a client stating that I was pleased to report that the portfolio had increased in value by a certain percentage during the preceding quarter and that this performance had exceeded a lesser percentage increase in the Dow Jones Average (or perhaps it was the S&P Index). Back came my letter with a big black line drawn through the part relating to relative performance with the notation: "*Never* discuss relative investment performance with clients! What do you say when the account underperforms the market? Once you start there is no stopping." In defense of this seeming stodginess, my supervisor remarked to me that the objectives of each account were very different from the market index. Some had low-cost stock that effectively locked them into certain holdings, other holdings were "sacred cows" in the client's eyes for some reason or other. Some had high income requirements, and we weren't allowed to invade principal. There were innumerable valid reasons why a comparison with an unadjusted market index was unfair. I think this is something that today most individuals have forgotten in the mad rush to beat the market.

The most interesting account assigned to me by Messrs. Brown Brothers Harriman & Co. was that of Miss Greta Garbo, the reclusive and glamorous film star. I was told that this was one of three accounts Miss Garbo maintained, the others being at the Morgan Bank (naturally) and The Bank of New York. So we were in a horse race of sorts, even though Brown Brothers disdained to compare its market performance with market indices. As I write this, it occurs to me that my claim of seminal credit for DLJ in inventing the concept of multiple, competitive portfolio managers misses the mark. Greta Garbo had this idea long before. Was this where I picked up the idea of using competitive managers?

In any event, I never got my moment of glory, which was to have a tête-à-tête lunch with Miss Garbo, complete with Brown Brothers's ritual glass of sherry. I unwisely announced my decision to leave BBH & Co. (to form DLJ) a week or so before the great luncheon at which I had been scheduled to make my debut before Miss Garbo. BBH & Co. suggested it would be more discreet if I did *not* attend the luncheon inasmuch as I was leaving. Of course they were right, but I always regretted missing this luncheon with Greta Garbo.

Fast-forward nearly 40 years. It's now 1996 and once again I'm resigning from something. This time it's as chairman & CEO of an investment complex that manages more than $200 billion in assets, mostly for large institutional accounts that make Miss Garbo's account look like small potatoes. Performance measurement is now enshrined as a god (probably even at Brown Brothers), intense competition rages between competitive money managers, since new cash flow quickly moves toward hot investment performance. The total-return concept is accepted everywhere, even at some staid universities or charitable endowments who think nothing of spending 5 or 6 percent of the current market value of their endowments even though the real dividend and interest income may be only 2 or 3 percent. Most of them move in a herd (shepherded over by the likes of Cambridge Associates). If they stumble, they can all point to being in good company— "Harvard, Yale, Princeton, and other sacred names did the same thing, so don't blame us." This attitude always reminds me of a modern-day Japanese saying that was fashionable a few years ago in the Tokyo stock market, until it backfired: "If we all cross the street against the red light, no one gets hurt!"

I am not sure the contrarian approach to investing is any longer applicable to the management of today's institutional capital. That's why I've titled this chapter "The Demise of Contrarian Investing." The pressures for short-term investment performance are so great that a contrarian approach, which means going against the herd, becomes very risky to the personal well-being of the portfolio manager. The trader's mentality—"trend is your friend"—has unfortunately migrated to the level of the institutional portfolio manager, supposedly the top of the pyramid of investment decision making. Following, or climbing aboard, a trend already under way seems to hold the promise of instant investment performance.

This is based on the old law of physics: things in motion tend to stay in motion. Going against the trend—the contrarian way—usually takes time and patience to pay dividends.

Jeff Vinik, who had a superlative long-term track record in managing the huge Magellan Fund, an almost impossible task, found this out when he decided it was prudent to put 30 percent of the fund into U.S. Treasury bonds and notes following a year in which his fund had appreciated in value by nearly 40 percent. This didn't seem like such a dumb thing to me—I did it in my own IRA portfolio. But the fact that the stock market continued to go up another 10 percent over the next few months, while his bonds slipped a bit in value, brought the wrath of the gods down on him. He is no longer running Magellan or even at Fidelity. There may have been extenuating circumstances, but I suspect he'd still be on the job if stocks had gone down and underperformed the bond market.

The last great institutional contrarian manager—John Neff who piloted the Wellington Fund so successfully for many years by buying out-of-favor stocks—has recently retired. In his early 60s he was certainly entitled to retire with honor after so many good years. But even his relative performance had begun to slip a bit in recent years under the onslaught of trend-following, relentlessly bullish young investors. Among the sillier studies I've seen lately is one purporting to show that young portfolio managers do better than their older counterparts. I submit that the time period is too short, all in a rising market, to reach such a conclusion.

There is another more insidious constraint that prevents modern-day institutional portfolio managers from acting like contrarians—and that is the big role consultants play in deciding which firms are chosen to manage institutional assets. A later-day outgrowth of DLJ's (or Greta Garbo's) pioneering the concept of multiple managers of funds was the emergence of a brand new industry—investment *consulting*. The consultants don't actually manage money themselves (most never have), but they stand ready to tell you who should manage your funds. Their specialty is monitoring the thousands of different small money managers that are now flourishing in the United

States (talk about an industry ripe for a shakeout!). In truth
there is a need for such a service, though I think it would be
more useful if they spent more time on overall portfolio strategy and asset allocation rather than chasing the latest hot
money managers. To do what I think they should do would
require a different kind of consultant, more of a "Dutch
uncle" sort who might bring perspective to this frenetic chasing of investment performance.

The consultants don't like it when a money manager strays
from the style of investing to which the consultant has
assigned them. If you are considered a small growth-stock
investor, you don't dare buy General Motors (or any other
stock that is outside the assigned mold) no matter how cheap
it looks. The consultants have selected the manager because
of the firm's presumed prowess in a certain set style of investing, such as large-capital growth stocks, emerging "small cap"
growth stocks, cyclical stocks or "market timers" (not too popular these days), asset allocation, global, etc. "Alternative
investments" (which sound suspiciously like "alternative
lifestyles") are the consultants' latest hot button. In theory a
contrarian like me should like this but not at this late stage of
the market. My point is that everyone has their assigned niche
and is not expected even to *think* about straying from it. After
all, this is the age of specialization.

The result, of course, is to put blinders on the intelligence
of the portfolio manager, confining the manager to one set
style of investing. A portfolio manager for small-cap, emerg-
ing-growth stocks, for example, need never bother considering
relative values, such as whether some other category of investing might offer better value. Instead, it's a case of damn the
torpedoes, full-speed ahead. No matter how outrageously
priced small growth stocks have become, the manager effectively is forced to keep piling more money on an already overpriced group. Intelligence is abdicated. Of course, one could
close the fund to new subscriptions, which is sometimes done,
but it would be highly unlikely that the portfolio managers
would put more than 10 percent of the funds into cash equivalents. That would be to commit the sin of market timing,

which is so out of favor. So it became a case of "Damn the torpedoes, full-speed ahead."

In contrast, in the real world there is a time and season for everything. There is a rhythm to the markets—a time to be investing in small growth companies (usually when there is a shortage of growing earnings), a time for big blue chips, a time to put part of your money overseas, a time to be on the sidelines, even a time for bonds. Some think there is never a time for bonds, but even they have their place and time. They actually have done well in recent low-inflation years but still get "no respect."

The real dragon that has slain the contrarian investment managers, however, has been the long bull market in common stocks. Contrarians, I have found, are at their best when times are tough, when everyone else has run for cover. That's when the really great investment buys become available. These kinds of opportunities really haven't come along in the stock market since 1987, when the market was evidently overextended and spooked by a small increase in interest rates (showing how little bad news it takes to topple an overextended bull market). The resulting 23 percent drop in the Dow Jones average opened up some extraordinary buys. But that sell-off was of very short duration, so short it reinforced the popular view that stocks only go up.

It is difficult for any true contrarian to be bullish on the U.S. stock market today. That, of course, doesn't mean the market can't go up further, because the market always goes to extremes, on the upside and the downside. But the reality is that stocks, as measured by the Dow Jones Industrial Average, have compounded at a remarkable 15 percent *annual* rate of growth for the past decade.

This market appreciation far surpasses the so-called fundamentals. The economy isn't growing at anything like that rate—2 to 3 percent per annum is more likely. Corporate profits have been growing at a 7 to 8 percent rate since 1988— about half the annual rate of growth in stock prices. Granted, some catch-up to long-term trends was overdue following subpar market performances during the decade of the 1970s.

Even so, by all conventional statistical measures—market price to earnings per share, or dividends, or book value per share—the stock market at the beginning of 1997 appeared to be fully priced or overpriced. If you are a true long-term investor like Warren Buffett, I suppose there's no reason to sell. Unfortunately, inexperienced investors tend to lose their nerve during protracted downturns in the market.

The bottom line is that you, as an investor, can no longer count on institutional investors to provide contrarian investment management. They are programmed to drive right off a cliff because of their mandate to stay fully invested. This means that you have to become your own contrarian.

COMMON SENSE AND COMMON STOCKS

If the bad news is that contrarian investment management is dead, the good news is that individuals have been empowered (there's that word again) to make their own decisions as to how their retirement savings are invested. Just as the federal government would dearly love to find ways to get out of paying your Social Security (since the system seems headed for insolvency when the baby boomers start to retire en masse), so are big corporations in full retreat from their former willingness to offer large, inflation-adjusted pensions to their employees upon retirement. So-called defined-benefit (read, pension) plans are being replaced by "defined-contribution plans," in which the company agrees to set aside a certain sum each year for your retirement. But *you* are now empowered to decide how your nest egg is to be invested. In the past, most of the nation's retirement savings were managed by professional pension managers, who determined what percentage should be in stocks, bonds, real estate, etc.

This has profound significance for the future. For starters, most Americans aren't even remotely equipped by training and experience to make such important investment decisions. Increasing numbers, having heard of the miracle of the stock market, which is believed to have returned 9 percent a year throughout the twentieth century, are simply opting to put their 401K plans or other retirement savings in one of the well-known common stock mutual fund groups such as

Fidelity or Vanguard. This has worked well so far, perhaps even becoming a self-fulfilling prophecy. Remember the Japanese saying, "If we all cross against the red light at the same time, no one gets hurt."

Individuals have also withdrawn funds from bank thrift accounts and reinvested the proceeds in mutual funds. Recently I had occasion to give a speech on trends in the financial services industry. Even I was shocked to note that all types of savings accounts, certificates of deposit, etc., at banks have had virtually no growth over the past seven years—less than 1 percent growth per annum. By contrast, the mutual funds have grown at 22 percent per annum during the same period. Mutual fund assets are now 1.5 times total bank thrift accounts; a decade ago things were reversed: bank savings deposits were 2.5 times larger than mutual fund assets. If all this helps explain the New Era stock market that seemingly goes up and up, the important point to remember is that *you* are now in charge of your destiny. Just because you picked well-known mutual funds with long track records of excellent performance doesn't mean that they will be able to save you if the stock market has a bad sell-off, which sooner or later it will. As discussed in the previous chapter, the institutional fund managers are all programmed to keep driving straight ahead. And the index funds must buy as long as their cash flow is positive—no matter how overpriced the market.

What that says to me is that *you* have to be the contrarian. When I say "you," I'm thinking largely of the mass of individual investors who are now empowered to decide what to do with their retirement funds. However, I think those CEOs and other officers of large corporations who have exited defined-benefit pension plans in favor of defined contributions, and delegated investment choices to the individual participant, need to give some careful thought as to whether these chickens might come back home to roost if things don't go well in the stock market. In the event of a catastrophic stock market drop (and I hope we never have one again like the 1930s), it seems inconceivable that American corporations will not feel some responsibility (or have it forced back on them) to help their retirees who have been wiped out. If that is a possibility, and history has a way of repeating, companies would be wise to encourage their employees to build some safety nets that are not solely dependent on the stock market.

Can all this pessimism be coming from one of the authors of *Common Stock and Common Sense* 40 years ago? I don't really see it as pessimism but rather realism. It's time for a new manifesto in which I would put common sense first, hence the title of this chapter "Common Sense and Common Stocks."

Just as I wouldn't even *try* to tell you how to beat the market or even suggest that it's time to get out of the stock market, I do have a few common sense nostrums that have helped me live peacefully with bull markets and the occasional bear markets that come along.

First, start by admitting to yourself that you don't really know what the market is going to do. This applies to the stock market, the bond market, commodities, real estate, or whatever. Maybe I'm a slow learner, but I've observed the markets closely for more than 40 years, and I still can't tell you how high is high or how low is low. The market always goes to extremes—the pendulum swings too far. Right now I think the stock market looks high, but I really don't know. I could have said that six months ago or two years ago. I have gained a great deal of humility by having watched the market for so many years. During the first 20 years of my career on Wall Street, it seemed like the Dow Jones would *never* get through 1000. For a decade (1972–1982), the stock market made absolutely no headway. This is difficult to comprehend for those who came into the business during the past 15 years when times have been so good (15 percent *annual* appreciation). I always have an opinion as to whether the market is high or low—but I have to admit to myself that I really don't know.

Second, never get completely out of the stock market. No matter how high it is, it can always go higher. If you get totally out of the market and it goes higher, you will become embittered and lose your perspective. On the other hand, even if you have only 10 percent of your assets in stocks, you can still enjoy the party. The Japanese have an amusing saying which I've always liked that pertains to investing, especially if you think the market is getting high: "Enjoy the party, but dance near the exit!" For mental health, as well as financial health, never get completely out of the stock market.

There is an old rule of thumb as to what percentage of your assets should be in stocks—and it's not so dumb. Subtract your age from 100 to get the percentage of your assets that should be in equities. My age is 67, which would indicate that I should have no more than 33 percent of my assets in stocks. Actually, I have 40 percent of my liquid assets in stocks, so I guess that makes me a bull even though I sound like a bear. By the way, I saw this rule quoted the other day in a newspaper article—except that the writer had modified it to "Subtract your age from 120 to get the right percentage in stocks"—a concession no doubt to today's bull market.

Third, don't put all your eggs in one basket. Here I have my own rule of thumb—I call it the Jenrette "one-third rule." One-third of your *total* assets (not just liquid assets) should be in stocks, one-third in bonds (or cash equivalent), and one-third in "real assets"—real estate being the best example, but I also lump in things like antiques and objets d'art under this third category. If you follow this formula, you should always have something working in your favor. The reverse, of course, also holds true—the bonds I own have hurt my performance lately. But I am *not* trying to beat the market. Preservation of capital, against the inroads of both inflation and bad markets, plus peace of mind are goals equally as important to me as capital appreciation.

The bonds and cash equivalents are held for a worse-case scenario—depression, deflation, bankruptcies. Ask the Japanese if you don't believe these things can happen again in modern times. That's why I prefer U.S. Treasury bonds—not only are they highly liquid but there's no credit risk (or at least I thought so until the Republicans, supposedly defenders of the nation's credit, recently threatened to default on the federal debt). The U.S. Treasury together with the Federal Reserve, effectively has the power to print money, something corporate borrowers cannot do, so the credit is good, as long as you don't mind being repaid in dollars. I am less keen on municipal bonds—especially since the virus of Orange County, California's default (despite being one of the richest counties in the nation) could spread, especially in bad times when you expect your bond portfolio to protect you. Municipals are also relatively illiquid and have less call protection. Stick to Treasuries, pay your taxes, and sleep well.

You should own real assets, especially real estate, for the opposite reason—an overheated economy and inflation. Most of us own real estate for our own housing, and that gives you a double benefit. It's hard for an individual investor to own a diversified portfolio of real estate, though some of the recently formed real estate investment trusts seem to have good potential despite the bad history of REITs. For most of us, if we add up our principal residence, perhaps a vacation home, some antiques or art collections, other furnishings and household equipment, you may discover you already have about a third of your net worth in "real things." I have a lot of antiques, paintings, and other objets d'art as part of my personal net worth. My "income" on them is the enjoyment I derive from them. Yet their value has easily kept up with the stock market over my lifetime. If you're still short on inflation hedges, throw in some gold, the classic inflation hedge which has lagged for the past 15 years, but would come alive if serious inflation returns.

That leaves the final third of your net worth in common stocks, which tend to do well in between the extremes of inflation and deflation. For most of us, accessing a professional manager through a mutual fund or variable life insurance or variable annuities, which can now be invested in common stocks as well as bonds, is the best solution. It's difficult to get much attention on an individually managed account unless you have at least $1 million.

A footnote to "don't keep your eggs all in one basket." Use more than one custodian, preferably in a different geographic location. I keep some of my money in North Carolina at the Wachovia Bank—it's so conservative, so safe and geographically removed from New York, where I keep the rest of my funds. Because everything is computerized today and systems can go down for a variety of reasons (fires, earthquakes, bombs, floods), you could be left without resources for an extended period. I learned this when being without power during several hurricanes—once for an entire month. This is a risk none of us likes to think about, but it is not prudent to keep everything in one location.

Fourth, make sure you have a "safety net" in place to provide steady income if your investments stumble. Your safety net can include Social Security, which I assume will be paid to the needy, if not the affluent. Your safety net could also include any company pension should you be fortunate enough to still have one. Next comes the income on your investments in those bonds and some income on stocks. But beyond this, I believe many people retiring in the future will conclude they need still more by way of guaranteed fixed income. This could be achieved by purchasing a lifetime annuity, a greatly underrated and misunderstood product. It's a shame the industry can't come up with a more understandable and less technical name than annuity, which is a turnoff to many savers.

I believe lifetime annuities, sold principally by life insurers although others are entering the business, will be *the* financial product of the future, replacing mutual funds, which have held sway for the past decade. It may take another decade, but eventually when the baby boomers start to retire, it will be a huge market. This is certainly a contrarian view given the much greater current popularity of mutual funds as a funding vehicle for retirement.

Why? First, investment returns accumulate tax-free in the annuity, until you start withdrawing the money. Today's variable annuities have options that allow the annuitant to choose between a wide variety of investment alternatives: stocks, small growth stocks, bonds, etc. Unlike a mutual fund where capital gains and income are taxed each year, taxes are deferred in the annuity until withdrawal. You can also shift from one funding alternative to another. If you have selected a common stock alternative and later decide you want to get out of the market, you can direct the company to put your funds in a money market account—all without incurring tax consequences as would be the case with mutual funds. This is a huge advantage.

Although some of these benefits are dissipated by higher sales and operating costs at the life insurance companies vis-à-vis mutual funds, this is gradually changing as the life companies become more efficient.

But the real reason I believe annuities are the product of the future has nothing to do with the tax-deferred benefits. Rather it is the unique right of the annuitant to elect to receive a lifetime guaranteed fixed monthly income upon retirement. This is an option most annuitants have not used in the past, partly because interest rates were high. Simply taking the principal in a lump sum and investing it in bonds or a savings account produced a satisfactory income. But in a lower interest rate environment, this might not produce enough income to live on. The other reason for their unpopularity was the fact that the choice of a lifetime annuity used to be irrevocable. Once you bought it, you were stuck even if your investment circumstances changed. Most people understandably like to keep their flexibility. Some life companies today, however, have come up with "market value adjusted" lifetime annuities which do allow you to change your mind and get your money back—or at least an adjusted amount. If interest rates have shot up, depressing bond prices, the value you would get back if you cancel the annuity is adjusted down correspondingly, much as if you had bought a long-term government bond (which in fact is what the companies invest the money in).

The advantage of a lifetime annuity is that if you live a long time it can bring you a much larger income than if you invested the money yourself. Why? The answer is the "mortality benefits," which may sound morbid, that accrue to those annuitants who live a long life. This is the "tontine-like" effect of an annuity—the benefits that would have been paid to those who die *before* normal life expectancy go to those who live *beyond* normal life expectancy. The winners are those who live a long time. The losers are those who die early, since benefits stop either immediately or after a certain period. There is usually no death benefit to survivors of the annuitant. Certainly if your health were poor at the time of retirement, you would not elect to take your proceeds as a lifetime annuity.

In recent years, it has become fashionable in buying life insurance to "buy term (insurance) and invest the rest." Term insurance has no cash surrender value and therefore is cheap on an annual premium basis. You are only paying for protection against premature death. It seems to me something similar could be said about a life annuity. "Buy a lifetime annuity with part of your retirement nest egg, and then invest the rest (with less worry because you now have a fixed-income safety net for the rest of your life)." In effect, you are insuring against the risk of living too long and outrunning your savings.

As companies continue to withdraw from fixed pensions and Social Security is called into question, I believe many individuals (as well as corporations getting out of the pension business) should give serious consideration to laying in their own "safety net" through a guaranteed lifetime annuity. Interestingly, at the end of World War II, U.S. corporations used to buy life annuities to fund their pension obligations before inflation and rising stock prices made them unfashionable as funding vehicles. Now may be a good time for some individuals to construct their own pension plan by putting a *portion* of their retirement funds into a life annuity.

Proceeds to purchase the lifetime annuity should come out of the one-third of your assets targeted for bonds, under my rule of thumb. Fixed-income annuities don't help, however, if big inflation returns. But they are the only way I know to be absolutely certain you never run out of income during your lifetime.

The prospect of increased longevity also makes the lifetime annuity more attractive as baby boomers start to worry about the "risk of living too long," and outrunning their savings. Interestingly, the life insurance companies are uniquely positioned to underwrite the possible risk of annuitants outliving their life expectancy. To the extent that happens, the life insurance companies would benefit from reduced mortality on their existing book of life insurance, cushioning the negative effect of larger than expected payments on guaranteed lifetime annuities.

Tontines, which were similar to life annuities, were a very popular way to save money at the beginning of the twentieth century. People were worried about having no income if they lived to an old age. Insurance regulators later outlawed tontines for somewhat fuzzy religious objections, such as the seeming immorality of someone benefiting from the death of other policyholders. The reasons, which are too complex to go into here, never made much sense to me, as I read history (I wasn't around then!). But inherently, life insurance against the financial risk of living too long makes just as much sense as insuring against the risk of premature death. I believe life annuities are the best hope for the life insurance industry to regain lost market share to mutual funds.

I'm afraid I've slipped back into my life insurance sales pitch, despite being retired. What I really wanted to do in this chapter was to emphasize that individuals, more than ever before, are in charge of their own destiny when it comes to investing their life savings. The problem is that you can't count on the professional money managers to tell you when to get in and out of the market. They are programmed to stay fully invested, regardless of their own feelings about the market. I believe it's too risky just to close your eyes and blindly put everything into stocks, even though that has worked extraordinarily well for the past 15 years. That's why I opt for a balanced strategy of diversifying investments.

Over the long term, I have found my one-third rule has worked well. My real estate, antiques, and art objects have appreciated about as much as the stocks, although there have been dips and cycles. Because most of my bond investing was done after the mid-1980s when interest rates peaked, they have also provided low double-digit returns while giving me considerable peace of mind, but I don't kid myself that these kinds of returns are sustainable long term.

I believe your money should give you peace of mind instead of causing you worry, as is so often the case. If you follow my guidelines, don't even bother to think about comparing your performance against the market averages. Brown Brothers had it right. Maybe you could compare every 10 years or so, but don't worry about year-to-year comparisons with the market. Part of your return should come in the peace of mind you have in knowing that you are about as well-hedged as possible against all eventualities. Sleeping well is the best revenge!

EVERYBODY SHOULD HAVE A HOBBY

Everybody should have a hobby. Why? First, because you find something that interests you. Second, because it's an important part of being "centered," or keeping "on an even keel," as we used to say. Or, as Dan Lufkin put it, "We mustn't forget that the whole purpose is to get a *return on life*." That is a profound bit of wisdom that many people either forget or never really think about as they rush about coping with crises. In today's profit-driven, bottom-line-oriented world, I suppose this now qualifies as a contrarian view. It also makes for long-distance runners rather than sprinters, whose business careers burn out at an early age. Lufkin is still happily doing deals and finding interesting small growth companies at age 65. Bill Donaldson seems happy back at DLJ as a senior adviser. Both have many outside interests and pro bono causes as well as favorite hobbies.

I consider having some sort of hobby or outside interest to be a key element in having a happy, stable life. No, I can't recall ever even being close to "cracking up," only to be rescued by thoughts of my hobby. But over and over during periods of stress at the office, I was able to gain a brief respite, or some solace, as a result of my hobby—which happens to be buying and restoring old houses of architectural merit, then filling them with antique furniture and furnishings of the period.

Having a hobby is certainly not a substitute for either a happy home life or a happy business life. Clearly we need both: people who love us and whom we love and a job that is satisfying and fulfilling. But a hobby or outside interest can be quite helpful in keeping one's marital or personal life, as well as one's business life, moving smoothly ahead. Having a hobby shared by both spouses clearly creates one more bond. In my case, I've even managed to foist my hobby off on DLJ and Equitable, witness the large collections of antiques, paintings, and decorative flourishes that embellish our offices. Happily, they've proved to be good investments, not just ornaments. They've also added a certain cachet, which is one more way that DLJ and Equitable are different from their peers.

But I'm afraid I'm making having a hobby sound like a dose of medicine, something you have to take to prevent your marriage or business career from coming under stress. No. The real reason for having a hobby lies in the enjoyment and satisfaction that it can bring you. Gardening, I am now learning, is a good example. Seeing all those green things spring to life or watching trees I planted 20 years ago burst into giants is very satisfying. Fishing, hunting, golfing, playing bridge, or doing magic (like my friend Ace Greenberg, who also makes financial magic at Bear Stearns) all can be relaxing and fun. Inevitably the hobby introduces you to a different circle of friends that you would not encounter in the normal course of events. If you're really good at your hobby, it might also bring you added fame or recognition.

While I didn't get into collecting old houses and antiques for either fame or financial gain, it's also nice to have a hobby where one can rationalize what otherwise might seem like frivolous spending. Art and antiques have proved to be rewarding investments over the years, as have the old houses I restored.

So why not find a hobby that can be financially rewarding as well as fun? For some people not in the investment business, investing money in the stock market can be an interesting—if sometimes dangerous—hobby. If pouring over potential investments pleasurably stimulates you or distracts your mind from the cares of your normal life or business, why not go for it? Certainly many older people get a great deal of fun and mental stimulation out of managing their investments. It's a way to stay connected to the world. A reminder though that this heart-warming 15 percent annual appreciation in stocks we've had for the past 15 years can't go on forever! But having investing as a hobby might also allow you to develop a defensive strategy that might protect some of your assets when the inevitable day of reckoning comes. As I pointed out in the preceding chapter, you can no longer look to the investment professionals to tell you when to get out of the market. In our new "empowered" world you must look to your own common sense first to protect your vital interests.

One nice thing about my collection of old houses, art, and antiques is that I don't have to "mark them to market" every day as I do my portfolio of marketable securities. Yet I know, from sales of comparable items, that they have appreciated tremendously in value over the past 30 years since I became a collector. But for me, this is just a form of lagniappe, something extra thrown in that I didn't count on or expect.

I feel strongly one should *not* buy old houses, art, or antiques just because they might turn out to be good investments. If they do not go up in value, you can still justify your collection on the pleasure and enjoyment it gives you. To me this is the "income" on my collections of art and antiques. I would do it all over, even if there were no residual value. And, of course, that could be the case again. If hard times return, such as the Depression, there will not be many buyers for my classical houses, which will look more like white elephants, or for the Duncan Phyfe antiques either.

I wish I could tell you how to develop a hobby or outside interest if you don't have one. For most of us, it just happens. But if you haven't found one, I urge you to try a little harder. Even if you don't feel a need for a hobby right now, I guarantee you will later, especially when retirement time comes.

My greatest benefit and enjoyment from my 30-year hobby of collecting old houses and antiques actually has come following my retirement as chairman of The Equitable and DLJ. There is an obvious, underrated shock at no longer having thousands of people and billions of dollars of assets (other people's money) at your beck and call, at least technically. But whether you are a CEO or someone more in the ranks, there is still an obvious shock effect when you wake up to realize a big part of your life—your business career—has ended. If you have some strongly developed outside interests, they can go a long way toward mitigating the shock effect and helping you enjoy your new-found freedom. All those grandchildren you've been looking forward to spending time with may not want to play with you, but your hobby will always be there for you to enjoy.

CONTRARIAN THINKING VERSUS CARTESIAN LOGIC

As I sat by the river recently, I began to contrast the contrarian way of thinking I have described, which comes natural to me, with Cartesian logic (or *logique*), so beloved by most of my many friends who are French. Although logic-driven, judgmental thinking, of course, is not limited to the French, they seem to articulate it better. As I have noted previously, Equitable's Corporate Management Committee under my predecessor was populated with Promethians, who according to the personality tests they were given, were all judgmental, logical, very traditional in their thought processes—all eminently Cartesian! I was the one exception, a maverick who reacted differently and put more weight on perceptions and intuition.

Not having been educated in France, I don't know quite how the French became so imbued with Cartesian *logique*, but most seem to be. The French have a word *donc*, which means "therefore," that I clearly hear them using, even with my inadequate French, over and over as they make points in espousing a course of action. An observation (A) is noted and presented as self-evident, *therefore (donc)* the speaker moves to observation (B), which *therefore (donc)* leads logically to (C) and so on to an inevitable, irrefutable, inescapable *donc* conclusion. The closest training I had to Cartesian logic in school was geometry, where we were taught to "prove" everything by citing elaborate axioms and postulates, such as "Things equal to other things are equal to each other," etc.

Despite having been a pretty good geometry student long, long ago, my contrarian mind seems naturally to work *backward*. That sounds like a horrible confession! The light bulb comes on, the idea or new insight suddenly dawns on me. This is not as capricious as it sounds, however, because the insight or idea does, after all, emanate—somehow—from long years of experience, like a warning instinct. After this flash of insight comes to me, usually triggered by something someone says or what I see, I then try to work backward to try to piece together a trail of logic that would justify my conclusion. I have learned from experience that many people—especially the French (though not Claude Bébéar of AXA, who most certainly has a contrarian mind)—distrust these so-called flashes of insight that seem to come out of nowhere. If I am trying to sell an idea to a person or persons of this persuasion, I make a practice never to present my conclusion first, especially if it's at all daring or unconventional. That invites hostility, and warning alarms go up against some crazy new off-the-wall idea. Instead I proceed very methodically describing how I would have arrived at the conclusion under the step-by-step, scientific, sequential thinking that is Cartesian logic. In other words, I pretend I arrived at my conclusion by Cartesian logic.

I must confess, however, that I always prefer to hear the conclusion first when someone else is making a presentation to me. It drives me up the wall when someone drones on endlessly from A to B to C, all the while I am trying to guess where all this is leading. I have to resist an urge to say, "Get to the point," or "Where is all this leading?" or "What do you want me to do?" Perhaps I am simply too impatient to struggle through the long buildup of a case. I prefer to know the conclusion so I can test the hypothesis as we go along.

Despite my love for contrarian thinking and tolerance (if not belief) of what may seem to many like unscientific thinking (astrology, handwriting analysis, etc.), I have concluded that there really is not as much difference between contrarians and Cartesians as might seem to be the case. The contrarian who gets an idea like a flash of insight still must test it by working backward. Is it plausible? While I may appear to others to be acting on instinct, my decision is always based on an instant flashback that creates a logic trail that says to me the idea makes sense. The new piece of information, or insight, that has come to me unlocks the puzzle, changes the way I've been looking at things. It's like the discovery of the Rosetta Stone that finally unlocked the secret of Egyptian hieroglyphics. All the pieces of the puzzle suddenly fall in place. What seemed logical is no longer logical in light of the new insight.

Unless you believe in chaos theory (which I have examined only superficially), there is a case to be made for both my type of contrarian thinking and Cartesian logic. Ultimately there is no difference. It's all in how you get there. With perfect hindsight everything (or almost anything) can be explained by logic *if* only we had known some piece of missing information. While the contrarian may sometimes act on some sixth sense that does not seem very logical, the type of contrarian thinking I am advocating simply looks at things from a different angle but still aspires to be logical. This lets you work backward and reexamine the logic trail.

If contrarian thinking is really nothing more than working *backward* from a flash of insight to reach a logical conclusion while Cartesian logic works *forward* to a logical conclusion, then under my old geometry lesson (Things equal to other things are equal to each other.) there is no conflict between my contrarian thinking and Cartesian logic. Done right they both equal the same thing—the right answer, the right strategy. Both contrarians and Cartesians need to be more tolerant of the other's thought process.

MAKING A DIFFERENCE IN THIS LIFE

I have always been struck by what a difference one person can make in life, in an organization, group, or company. This runs counter to the popular belief that things are run by some sort of establishment, that the individual can't make a difference, so why try? Most people admittedly don't have the desire or temperament to try to move mountains, but I believe each of us does make a difference—for better or worse—even if its just limited to one's own family, friends, or immediate surroundings. And I am *absolutely* convinced, both from personal experience and watching others in action, that a single dedicated human being—with conviction and will power—can be the catalyst for totally transforming an organization.

Over and over, I've seen moribund companies or organizations come alive under inspired leadership, which usually can be traced to one person who is a true believer, who unleashes the potential. Similarly, I have seen bad leadership by one person at the top totally demoralize an organization in a short period of time. The power of one person to make such a difference for good or bad is awesome.

This, of course, doesn't mean that the "one person" has to do it all alone. No manager is less effective than the one who tries to do everything by himself or herself. You have to enlist others in your crusade. The leader sets the tone, the direction. Then you need to get out of the way, avoid micromanaging. Being nondirective is better than highly directive when you are working with at least reasonably intelligent people. If you aren't, nothing said here will solve your problems!

The real key to leadership is that you have to give credit and recognition to others when they succeed in whatever you've asked them to accomplish. If they don't succeed, take the blame yourself. After all, you selected them for the job. If you are willing to give credit to others, there is no limit to what you can achieve in this world. Conversely, if *you* don't give them credit, they will take credit for themselves anyway, and your leadership will soon be eroded.

As we look around us, it is clear that some people are builders and some people are "takers." The takers exploit companies, draining them, sucking them dry, and casting them aside. They do the same thing with people—using them, exploiting them, not helping them develop, eventually abandoning them with no regard for the individual's welfare. I can spot users and takers a mile away and try to steer clear of them.

There seems to be a growing belief in the world today that being a taker is the way to succeed financially. Being a contrarian, I beg to disagree. It's better to be a builder. More great fortunes have been made by the many builders of this world than a few well-publicized takers. But it's also morally the right thing to do.

> By trying to do the right thing, whether it's helping educate your fellow citizens or make the world a little more beautiful, you should try to wear the white hat, be on the side of the angels....And the wonderful thing about that is that it usually ends up rebounding on you.—Richard Jenrette (*The New York Times*)

This quote, whose syntax admittedly leaves something to be desired, nevertheless represents an accurate portrayal of my philosophy of life. The statement was made by me during an interview with a *New York Times* reporter at least a decade ago. A friend saw my quote in the *Times* and was so taken with it that he had it inscribed on a silver plaque and sent to me as a gift. I keep it on a counter in my bedroom (along with all those yellow sheets of nocturnal worries that I have accumulated over the years). Looking at this quote is a nice daily reinforcement of the idea that we should all try to be on the side of the angels.

The only thing I would change about the quote, aside from the rambling syntax, is the suggestion at the end that all this "do good" philosophy is commercially driven—that doing the right thing pays. I sincerely believe this to be the case, but I would have preferred to end the quote with my even more firmly held belief that you should do the right thing anyway, regardless of whether or not it pays off on the bottom line.

I have always held to the view that, in everything you attempt, you should try to leave things better than you found them. I have tried to do this with every organization that I have belonged to—from schools attended to charitable and fraternal organizations, and, of course, at the three companies that I have worked with so closely, DLJ, Alliance Capital, and The Equitable. I believe I have left each of them strong financially, well-managed, and heading "onward and upward." The only organization I ever belonged to on which I have to admit making no impact was the U.S. Army. It was a good experience in discipline, but no place for a contrarian who likes to do things differently.

The same attitude of leaving things better than you found them should be true in your people relationships. The people I have hired and worked with over the years have done quite well in life, not necessarily for what I did but what they did for themselves. But I helped create an environment in which they could flower and that is very satisfying to me. It is a source of great satisfaction as I look over my business career.

Leaving things better than you found them doesn't necessarily mean you always have to change things. Sometimes all that is needed is restoration, not a complete new look or new direction. I've learned this in my hobby of restoring old houses. I've restored at least a dozen historic houses—150 to 200 years old—that were classical jewels in their prime. Often there were ugly additions appended that needed to be stripped away to get them back to their original, more pristine state.

Probably whoever put the addition on thought they were improving things, but so often they only succeeded in cluttering up or obliterating what was once beautiful.

In looking at a company, I always try to use the preservationist's eye to discover what was beautiful or enduring about the company (I suppose you could do this in helping rehabilitate people also). Despite my penchant for contrarian thinking, I am not one who believes in sweeping away all traditions or traditional ways of doing things. Where they have stood the test of time, better to leave them in place, polish them up and let them gleam again. Turn them to your advantage. You will have a much stronger company if you build on this foundation. Tradition can be a great thing, which is not to say that all traditions per se are good. But I am always very cautious about casting aside things that have stood the test of time.

At Equitable, a 140-year-old company, I found many traditions that perhaps were not quite what I would have done but which had stood the test of time. This included an organization of agency managers called *The Old Guard*. The Old Guard, named for Napoleon's elite troop, had been conceived nearly a hundred years ago at another time of strife for The Equitable. The Old Guard had been formed to defend Equitable's chief executive officer during this troubled period. They similarly rallied around me in my hour of need. Some of Equitable's agent-award ceremonies, such as the Order of Excalibur, seemed from another time, another place, and not "what's happening." (I had apparently gotten over my desire to build another Camelot.) Yet the agents loved the order and aspired to it. Far be it from me to take this away. I believe all great companies develop traditions. If they haven't, they aren't great. If you aspire to greatness, it's probably unwise to sweep away these traditions, which can be the foundation for something even more beautiful.

During the 1970s the United States went through a great catharsis. So many traditions were cast aside as not being relevant. One of the great lessons of life, however, is that everything does not have to be relevant. Charming irrelevancies and customs can make life more enjoyable and don't need to be cast aside.

When I bought my first house, a multicolumned Greek Revival classic in Charleston, South Carolina, I granted a life tenancy on one floor to Mrs. C. Norwood Hastie, whose family had owned the house. She was 76 at the time and lived to be 90—a long time for a life tenancy. I had no urgency to have the whole house, and it let me learn by observing some of the charming "irrelevancies" that made her life attractive. For example, every evening at about 6 p.m. she would dress for dinner, slipping on a very long (to the floor) dark blue or black velvet gown. Miriam, her maid, would bring her a glass of bourbon. Then Mrs. Hastie would hold court. Friends might drop in, but if none did, she still dressed for dinner anyway and she had her ritual cocktail, enjoying it and reading alone or enjoying the beautiful harbor view if there were no guests. I discovered that Mrs. Hastie was extremely well-read, au courant, and up-to-the-minute on everything going on in the world. Even though I was 40 years younger, it was fun to talk to her, and I learned a lot. She was a civilized human being in a world constantly endangered by barbarians at the gate.

For those of us who work in suits all day, "dressing for dinner" might mean putting on something casual. Too bad Roman togas never came back in style (at one point in the 1970s it seemed like they might)! The important thing is to be civilized—stop, shower, make yourself a cool drink (if you don't have a Miriam), and relax awhile. I had a much more helter-skelter life growing up, and I was glad to have the opportunity to observe the gracious way of living that Mrs. Hastie had decreed in her life. I try to follow Mrs. Hastie's example of taking a break at the end of each day, even though I may cook the dinner and wash the dishes.

My biggest frustration today is that so few people seem turned on to beauty, unless it's sex and the human body. Ugliness around us seems to be tolerated and taken for granted, or perhaps not even seen. This is a disappointing side of the baby-boomer generation that I had counted on to make the world more beautiful. But I haven't given up on them! This insensitivity to ugliness, for example, allows us to string electric, telephone, cable, and Lord knows what other kinds of wire—all in the name of being wired—along the most beautiful streets or in front of magnificent scenery. We seem to have regressed to the way things looked at the turn of the century when telephone and telegraph wires were strung all over the streets of New York, badly cluttering the views in every direction. Someone eventually had the sense to decree that they all had to go underground, probably a better solution economically as well as esthetically. Enough of complaining.

Try to leave things better than you found them. Try to do something beautiful in this world. Where did I get these weird ideas? Maybe in high school. I remember having to memorize lines from Keats's "Ode to a Grecian Urn."

> A thing of beauty is a joy forever. Its loveliness increases, it will never pass into nothingness.

Keats wrote those words over 175 years ago, shortly before his premature death at age 26. But his lines have descended to us and will go on and on. I keep thinking that if I create or help create something beautiful, it just might last forever. I believe in building for the ages, even though I won't be around forever. In my life I have enjoyed beautiful things built by those who came before—beautiful houses, great institutions. I feel obligated to help pass on some of these beautiful things to future generations.

Only a contrarian would dare to end a book on business management with poetry, but here's one more comforting thought from Robert Browning that I once had to memorize. It seems more relevant as we age.

> Grow old along with me!
> The best is yet to be,
> The last of life, for which
> the first was made.

I have found life gets better and better each decade. I've never had a desire to go back and relive an earlier period, even though I enjoyed them all. The best is yet to be. If you hitch your star to beauty and keep trying to do the right thing, life can be very sweet and satisfying.

PART FOUR

COMMON STOCK AND COMMON SENSE

Now may be a good time to revisit *Common Stock and Common Sense*, the small booklet first published in 1959 as DLJ's opening salvo in introducing the new firm. History has a way of repeating. Thirty-seven years later, investors once again have been lulled into believing that all one has to do to achieve extraordinary investment performance is to buy the Standard & Poor's 500 Index. Small growth stocks, of the type favored by DLJ at its founding, have lagged in the market as money pours into index funds. When the founders of DLJ wrote *Common Stock and Common Sense*, they argued that investors would have to seek out future blue chips—smaller, still unrecognized growth companies—for gains comparable to what they had experienced simply by buying the market averages in the 1950s. The past is prologue!

Common Stock and Common Sense

DONALDSON, LUFKIN & JENRETTE
INCORPORATED
Members New York Stock Exchange
51 BROAD STREET
NEW YORK 4, NEW YORK

Common Stock and
Common Sense

THE RECORD of remarkable capital gain performance by "blue chip" common stocks over the past ten years has fostered optimistic investor expectations of similar gain in the next ten years.

By any measure the performance of these leading U. S. industrial stocks during the post-war period has been remarkable. As of June, 1959, anyone who had invested equal amounts in each of the 30 stocks comprising the Dow-Jones Industrial Average at mean market prices prevailing in 1949 would have experienced nearly a five-fold increase in the market value of his securities. Similar outstanding results could have been obtained by investing in Vicker's "Favorite Fifty" stocks of institutional investors or Standard & Poor's 500 Industrial Stock Average.

In view of this performance, the great reliance placed by many investors and investment managers on the "blue chips" cannot be considered surprising. The normal tendency is to project such past gains into the future, with the result that a portfolio of leading U. S. industrial stocks is widely regarded as a relatively riskless route to large capital gain.

Are these expectations of future capital gain possibilities realistic? Can today's investor simply buy the "blue chips" and achieve

1

general market appreciation on the order of the past ten years? While there is no intention here to say that some further gain will not be realized in the "blue chip" area, there are grounds for believing that expectations of future gain based on the record of the past decade are unrealistic.

The most significant change in the position of the 1959 investor *vis à vis* the 1949 investor is in the multiple of earnings reflected in common stock prices today. Today's "Favorite Fifty" stocks are selling at price-earnings ratios which average 21 times estimated 1959 earnings. Ten years ago these same stocks could have been purchased at prices averaging 7.7 times 1949 earnings.

The significant fact this marked widening of price-earnings ratios has tended to obscure is that corporate per share earnings have experienced no more than a relatively moderate growth in the past decade. Whereas today's "Favorite Fifty" *stocks* have appreciated in market value over six-fold from their mean average prices prevailing in 1947-49, *earnings* for these same companies on the average have only slightly more than doubled in this period.

The table below illustrates the much more rapid rate of growth in market values *vs.* per share earnings for Vicker's "Favorite Fifty":

(Index 1947-49 = 100)

	1949	1950	1951	1952	1953	1954	1955	1956	1957	1958	1959(E)
Mean Ave. Market Prices	102.0	135.8	182.7	202.7	202.7	269.4	357.3	436.9	447.9	495.3	613.8
Mean Ave. Earnings Per Share	100.5	135.2	129.1	127.1	140.0	130.2	202.7	206.7	206.7	189.0	222.4
Price x Earnings Ratio	7.7	7.9	10.8	12.3	11.4	13.3	14.2	15.8	16.3	20.2	21.0

The performance of certain so-called "growth" industries illustrates this fact even more dramatically. Two such industries are paper and rubber:

2

PAPERS AND PAPER PRODUCTS*
(Index 1947-49 = 100)

Average Sales Performance

1949	1950	1951	1952	1953	1954	1955	1956	1957	1958	1959-E
102	126	154	152	181	204	246	263	261	265	275

Average Profit Performance (Before Taxes)

1949	1950	1951	1952	1953	1954	1955	1956	1957	1958	1959-E
97	140	162	150	171	184	235	235	193	176	210

Stock Performance—(Average Price-Earnings Ratio)

1949	1950	1951	1952	1953	1954	1955	1956	1957	1958	1959-E
5.0x	5.7x	8.3x	9.3x	9.1x	12.5x	15.0x	16.8x	17.7x	23.1x	20x

In the case of these seven major paper equities, the price-earnings ratio has advanced from 5 times to 20 times estimated 1959 earnings. Using net profit before taxes, profits have roughly doubled. As a result, adjusting pretax profit figures for per share increase, the group as a whole has advanced nearly eight times in market price over these past ten years.

---

* Includes Champion, Crown Zellerbach, International Paper, Kimberly-Clark, Rayonier, Scott Paper and West Virginia Pulp and Paper.

RUBBER AND RUBBER FABRICATORS*
(Index 1947-49 = 100)

Average Sales Performance

1949	1950	1951	1952	1953	1954	1955	1956	1957	1958	1959-E
93	123	157	161	171	161	202	212	225	227	235

Average Profit Performance (Before Taxes)

1949	1950	1951	1952	1953	1954	1955	1956	1957	1958	1959-E
76	182	277	226	226	180	257	248	239	227	235

Stock Performance—(Average Price-Earnings Ratio)

1949	1950	1951	1952	1953	1954	1955	1956	1957	1958	1959-E
5.3x	3.6x	5.0x	6.6x	6.1x	9.2x	10.2x	11.6x	12.6x	16.2x	16x

* Includes Firestone, Goodyear, Goodrich, U. S. Rubber and General Tire.

In the case of the five largest rubber equities, the price-earnings ratio has advanced from 4 times to 16 times estimated 1959 earnings (adjusting for depressed year earnings performance in 1949). Yet pretax earnings have only advanced 2¼ times. Adjusting pretax profit figures for per share increase, the group has advanced better than 8½ times in market price from 1949 to 1959.

There are a number of explanations for the willingness of investors to pay more per dollar of common stock earnings today. Fears of a serious Post-World War II depression which were prevalent in the latter half of the 1940s have been replaced by expectations of continued inflation, with a consequent diminishing of the relative attractiveness of fixed income securities. Other factors often mentioned to justify the present level of stock prices relative to earnings include increased outlays for research and development, expanded cash flow through larger and accelerated depreciation, new stability in cyclical industries through lower break-even points, the gradual buildup of capacity which only now can be reflected in larger earnings, expectations of a marked upturn in sales and earnings flowing from the projected rise in family formations, increased real income, and expanding worldwide demand during the next decade, and finally the much discussed shortage of "blue chip" common stocks which are in greatest demand by investors.

It is not our purpose here to attempt to justify the current level of price-earnings ratios, but merely to point out the breakdown of gain in market value between actual earnings growth and growth in the price-earnings ratios, whether justified or not.

Assuming the existence of some practical ceiling on price-earnings ratios, however, one might expect future growth in overall stock values to be more nearly in line with growth in corporate earnings. While opinions vary as to whether the next ten years will witness some further widening of price-earnings ratios, or conversely an actual contraction, a repeat performance of the past decade in which average price-earnings ratios have nearly tripled seems unlikely. Such a performance would necessitate average multiples of 60 times earnings which few investors today would consider a realistic possibility.

4

Thus it seems unreasonable to assume that today's investor can expect a growth in multipliers from current levels to yield dramatic stock market performance for most of the large industry leaders with no more than an historical rate of earnings growth ahead of them. Certainly some industry groups will come into greater market favor and show good gain—such as the steels during 1958-59—but overall levels of even "unfavored" groups today are relatively high and multiplier gains of 3 times to 4 times for any group seem remote.

Today's investor seeking comparable gain in the 1960s will not be able to buy the "Favorite 50", the industry leaders, which have already been bid up to high earnings' multiples in the process of reaching the "charmed circle". Comparable gain in the 1960s will come primarily through identifying the "Future Favorite 50"; stocks of companies which will benefit from the two-pronged effect of a large percentage earnings gain compounded in the company, with this gain compounded again by an increased price-earnings ratio in the market.

The problem of successfully identifying such companies breaks into two parts:

        1.   Where to look.

        2.   What to look for.

WHERE TO LOOK:

The most obvious place to look is where, for one reason or another, the majority of investors are not looking. This is usually in the over-the-counter or regional exchange markets. Most investors aren't looking here for a number of reasons:

  . . . A greater element of capital risk is arbitrarily attached to this area by the investor group in general.

  . . . Usually the limited number of shares available make large scale investigative and selling efforts less lucrative for the majority of investment firms. Often the limited number of shares available precludes broad use of the stock in the accounts and/or recommendations of the larger investment firms.

. . . Limited demand and following, as well as investment house interest, affects immediate marketability. In addition, the immediate purchase or sale of large blocks is difficult except under special circumstances.

. . . Size, and sometimes local nature, of the company limits general investor knowledge.

All of these objections are legitimate to some varying degree, but as with most tenets in the investment field, there is no black and white. A number of the smaller companies traded in this area, with sales usually ranging between 5 to 50 million dollars and with well established growth patterns, products, and markets carry a good deal less risk than size alone might imply, enjoy brisk if limited demand, can be purchased and sold in good volume in reasonable time and do enjoy some very sound and aggressive investment backing.

The very fact that people aren't generally looking in this area, however, frequently allows the stocks of such companies to be purchased at considerably lower earnings' multiples than their more widely known counterparts. In addition the larger percentage growth attainable on a smaller starting base often yields the superior sales and earnings performance desired, and such growth by definition soon moves the company into larger markets, expands the shares outstanding and available for trading, attracts investment interest and investors, begins to expand the multiplier, and tomorrow's "blue chip", institutional holding is discovered.

WHAT TO LOOK FOR:

The problem is to recognize a growth company at an early stage in development and to buy such a company at a reasonable multiple of earnings. First it is necessary to define a *growth company* and then a *reasonable* multiple of earnings.

. . . A Growth Company

To many people a growth company is any company whose stock goes up in price. As was pointed out above, however, in many cases this price rise has had little to do with actual company performance. What then is a growth company? There seem to be two general approaches to defining growth companies. For

6

lack of better terms, we shall call these the *quantitative* and *qualitative* approaches, although the two more often than not overlap and the distinction is mostly one of degree. Samuel L. Stedman of Carl M. Loeb, Rhoades and Company defines a growth company as one which is showing a 12-15% growth in per share earnings compounded yearly. J. Eugene Banks of Brown Brothers, Harriman and Company calls a growth company one whose per share earnings are trending upward more rapidly than the per share earnings of the more widely used averages. William B. Harris, writing for *Fortune Magazine,* calls a minimum definition of a growth company "a corporation whose earnings per share have shown an annual rate of increase, over several years, of more than 4% (in constant dollars) or 6.5% (in current dollars) which is about the annual growth rate of the U. S. economy during the postwar period".[1] Perhaps the earliest definition of this quantitative measurement of growth was expressed by Fred Y. Presley writing in the Annual Report of *National Investors Corporation* in 1938:

> "The studies by this organization, directed specifically toward improved procedure in selection, afford evidence that the common stocks of growth companies—that is, companies whose earnings move forward from cycle to cycle, and are only temporarily interrupted by periodic business depressions—offer the most effective medium of investment in the field of common stocks, either in terms of dividend return or longer term capital appreciation. We believe that this general conclusion can be demonstrated statistically and is supported by economic analysis and practical reasoning."

Although this group seems to lay major emphasis on compounded growth in earnings, qualitative analysis of the particular company in question also plays a part in the definition of a growth company. Mr. Harris, for example, lists a number of measurements to be applied to a potential growth company along with an emphasis on a particular growth rate. He includes the maturity of the industry, position in and type of markets served, dilution and dividend payout policies, company size in relation to its market, and alert management.

---

1. *Those Delicious Growth Stocks;* Fortune, April 1959.

Philip Fisher, West Coast investment advisor and author of *Common Stocks and Uncommon Profits,* lists 15 points to search for in a growth company.[1] Whereas Mr. Harris covers general areas in a company's internal and external operations, Mr. Fisher tends to go into much greater detail in the internal workings of a particular company, attempting to measure management determination at various levels of command, the type and quality of sales organization, labor and personnel policies, executive relations and depth, cost and accounting controls, incentives, individual product potentials, effectiveness of R&D work, as well as some of Mr. Harris' broader measurements.

Peter Bernstein, writing in the *Harvard Business Review,* while measuring increase in earnings over a given period of time, also succinctly elaborates on the view that "true growth is organic, comes from within, and is reflected in the creation of the company's own market".[2] Mr. Bernstein would subscribe to a number of the characteristics outlined for a growth company, but in all probability would hold that these characteristics are typical in any well-managed company, and that they in themselves do not distinguish a growth company. (A good example of Mr. Bernstein's "internal growth and market development" concept might be Polaroid Corporation.)

Our own experience has directed an emphasis on four main points when defining a growth company:

1. A steadily improving record of sales (recognizing unit as well as dollar sales), per share earnings, and to a lesser extent, profit margins. (Two excellent examples of companies which fulfill this requirement are Henry Holt and Haloid Xerox.)

   Any discussion of percentage or degree of improvement desired—the quantitative measurement—of necessity gets into price willing to be paid. The same can be said of the length of the record and the "quality" of the earnings; i.e.,

---

1. *Common Stocks and Uncommon Profits;* Harper Bros., copyright 1958 by Philip Fisher.
2. *Growth Companies* v. *Growth Stocks:* HBR, September-October, 1956.

the durability and stability of such earnings. One cannot put arbitrary figures on such measurements except in the very broadest sense and then, as with so much in the analysis of growth companies, the rest must be left to individual investor judgment. To establish an arbitrary rate of growth as a criteria for a growth *company*, as distinguished from a growth *stock*, disregards price. Whereas a company at a 10-15% rate of growth compounded may have demonstrated growth characteristics, at 30 times earnings the characteristics of that company's stock would show perhaps a less than desired result. At this high multiplier, in itself carrying extra risk, the stock above would double in 5-8 years given no further rise from a higher price-earnings multiple.

Return on net worth is not included in the above group as so much depends on the individual company's situation that this factor in itself cannot be viewed as a hard and fast measurement. Even the trend must be looked at in the light of changing circumstances—for instance the introduction of the rental option *vs.* direct sale will play havoc with return on net worth.

2. A good record of new product or process development and/or old product or process improvement resulting in sales volume generated in new markets or through a steadily growing share of existing old markets. (Examples might be American Photocopy, Papercraft, and Beauty Counselors.)

In a limited way the share of total company sales enjoyed by products no more than, say, five years old gives some indication of a company's ability along these lines. Equally important, however, is the sales end—the merchandising—marketing skills of a particular company. Indeed an exceptional marketing organization lends stability to a growth trend well beyond the weight many investors attach to it. Usually these two attributes—product or process development and strong marketing—go hand in hand for the most successful growth companies.

9

3. Management. In some measure the companies which fulfill Points 1 and 2 above will of necessity have a well above average management. Yet the successful growth stock investor cannot rely solely on the past to judge the future. He must make judgments as to the policies management is pursuing to achieve comparable future growth. He must become thoroughly familiar with the industry and related industries as well as the particular company in question to cover this point adequately. This is one of the most important investment considerations, and there is no short-cut the investor can take. Yet the rewards are large, and the investor who can satisfy himself on a management's future policies, and ability to implement these policies, has as close to a "sure thing" as one can ever find in the investment field.

4. Operating in an area characterized by rapid development of new applications and new products within an expanding overall market. (Examples might be Haveg Industries, Indiana Steel Products and Heli-Coil Corporation.)

To a degree this is the external application of Point 2. Once an investor has satisfied himself as to the first three points above, then the most promising company is one which is operating within a climate favorable to continued long term growth. (Such areas today might include plastics, electronics, light metals and so on.)

In addition, company size is an important factor in a growth company. Small size alone does not designate a growth company, but small size certainly should not arbitrarily disqualify a company from investment consideration. The relative size of a company must be measured against the background of the market and growth in the market served. (Point 4) Even more important the company itself should be measured first and foremost against the first three points outlined above.

10

It is a basic fallacy to assume automatically that a qualified smaller company cannot compete effectively with the larger companies in an industry. The flexibility and personal application that is more apt to be found in the smaller company in many cases far outweighs the greater resources of its larger competitors. The highly organized command levels, both staff and line, of some of our larger companies often slow the institution of new procedures, the creation, development and application of new ideas, and the implementation of new ways of approaching and solving problems. Given a strong nucleus of one to three capable men, personally involved through large stock ownership and initial creation, and concentrating on one particular area, a small company will out-perform and out-maneuver a good many of their larger, more diversified, many-tiered competitors.

Again the profitable research and development work that can be accomplished by these smaller companies in direct competition with larger competitors, and larger resources, is too often overlooked in the market. One has only to view some of the recent developments of General Ceramics ($7 million sales), Epsco ($8 million sales), and H. I. Thompson ($11 million sales) to gain confidence in the abilities along these lines of the qualified smaller company.

. . . A Reasonable Multiple of Earnings

Our second problem is that of defining a *reasonable* multiple of earnings. Basically a multiple of earnings reflects investor hopes for earnings' appreciation and dividend payout over a period of time. The multiple is also the market's appraisal of the degree of risk inherent in a particular investment—the durability and stability of earnings as well as projected earnings growth. Finally, the multiple of earnings reflects general investor confidence, or lack of confidence, in the economy as a whole.

The company whose stock is selling at a high price-earnings ratio is not necessarily overpriced. Indeed if Company A is growing at twice the rate of Company B then it might be argued that Company A is underpriced, other things being equal, if it is not selling at least twice the price of Company B. Given a long term rate of growth for Company A, there is no reason to assume that it should ever sell, again other things being equal, at less than double Company B's per share price. Yet this high price-earnings concept needs further examination.

There are a number of "formulas" which have been developed for appraising stock price outside of the conventional earnings multiplier approach. Among current favorites are the present worth concept of projected future earnings brought back to the present at a discount rate in proportion to judgment of risk involved or return desired, and the price x increase-in-earnings (past), or price x projected earnings (future) multiplier. Yet in applying all such formulas, a judgment must be made as to the rate of growth of *future* earnings and the degree of risk in these earnings. Above all else it is this judgment which is the key to a multiple of earnings. To justify a high multiple of earnings—over 20-25 times—one must have assured himself of the *four points* defining a growth company discussed above and must be able to see earnings compounding with little risk at an abnormal rate well into the future. Earnings must compound at an abnormal rate to realize the capital gain desired, for gain through an increase in multiplier has for the most part already occurred on the higher multiple stocks. A misjudgment of this future growth could not only fail to yield the desired gain but could result in some rather dramatic capital losses through a reduction in the multiplier. In addition, the risk involved with high multiple stocks may well lie beyond the investor's control. A general reversal of investor confidence usually tends to have a greater effect on those stocks which appear high on the basis of conventional multiplier analysis. This risk, however, is usually temporary in nature, and the investor who has done his homework well will come out satisfactorily over the longer term.

Yet it should be emphasized again that the high multiple stock must enjoy most of its future gain through a compounding of future earnings and not through an additional increase in the multiplier. Two similar companies—Haloid Xerox and American Photocopy—illustrate the importance of the multiplier for large capital gain investing. Below is a brief record of these two companies:

	AMERICAN PHOTOCOPY					HALOID XEROX			
	Sales	Per Share Earnings	Pretax Margin	Average P-E Ratio		Sales	Per Share Earnings	Pretax Margin	Average P-E Ratio
1952	$ 2.5M	$ .25	16.5%	—		$14.8M	$ .78	10.2%	14.5
1953	5.3M	.59	19.3%	—		15.8M	.79	10.8%	15.0
1954	7.2M	1.08	25.0%	—		17.3M	1.08	12.2%	43.0
1955	9.3M	1.36	24.5%	—		21.4M	1.51	12.4%	33.0
1956	12.2M	1.90	27.0%	—		23.6M	1.61	12.4%	30.0
1957	14.9M	2.31	26.5%	15*		25.8M	1.83	13.2%	34.0
1958	17.5M	2.71	26.5%	18		27.6M	1.96	13.5%	36.0
1959(E)	23.0M	4.20**	29.0%	28***		30.0M	2.30	13.8%	40.0***

* 1st year of public market.
** On the basis of 825,000 shares outstanding before 3-1 split.
*** January 1st, 1959-October 1st, 1959.

Earnings, sales and margin growth have been excellent in both companies (and incidentally these two companies qualify in other respects with our *four points* and are true growth companies). Yet during the 1958-59 period (the only comparison available as American Photocopy was first traded publicly in 1957) American Photocopy advanced from a low of 21 to a high of 151, or 7 times (readjusting for a 3-1 split), whereas Haloid Xerox advanced from a low of 47 bid to a high of 114 bid, or 2½ times. As can be seen, Haloid's multiplier could advance only slightly from an already high level whereas American Photocopy was definitely "reasonable" and could enjoy the two-pronged effect of increased earnings in the company and an expanded multiplier in the market.

Apparently American Photocopy was initially judged by the market to hold an undue degree of risk. This could have reflected the fear of strong, larger company competition and/or the small size of American Photocopy. (Minnesota Mining, Eastman Kodak, and Sperry Rand all are in the single copy reproduction field). Whatever the case, the degree of risk was misjudged by the market, and it was this misjudgment which allowed the astute investor to achieve such large capital gain.

13

Over the past year to 18 months a number of smaller, true growth companies have advanced in price to a point where one must seriously question the capital gain potential of their stock from present levels over the near to intermediate term. On the other hand, a few such high multiple companies are compounding earnings at such a rate, and with such a dramatic potential ahead of them for further growth with only limited risk, that their stocks will show excellent capital gain over the near to intermediate term.

CONCLUSION

The appreciation in average multipliers attached to the stocks of the larger "blue chip" companies over the past ten years has tended to obscure the more or less mediocre earnings growth in these companies. The price level of such stocks today would seem to rule out similar gain over the next ten-year period; indeed the multipliers attached to the "blue chips" in today's market could yield them quite vulnerable on the basis of only average projected earnings growth from an already large base.

For the most part investor misjudgment and lack of knowledge centers around the smaller companies, usually between $5 to $50 million annual sales, which frequently are traded over-the-counter or on a regional exchange. Primarily in this area are to be found the true growth companies—tomorrow's "blue chips" if-you-will —where dramatic capital appreciation can occur through compounded earnings on a relatively small base and advance in market stature as reflected by multipliers attached to such earnings. Here is where the astute capital gain investor can apply his theories of what constitutes a growth company and, with less risk than is generally realized, score excellent capital appreciation. And it is in this area that the tools of analysis and observation discussed above, the *four points,* can more readily be applied. If it is possible to fully understand and appraise an American Photocopy, the possibility of such an understanding and appraisal of an Eastman Kodak is a much more formidable task.

Mr. Thomas E. Brittingham, Jr. of Wilmington, Delaware, a private investor who year in and year out has surpassed every

14

published index of stock market performance, wrote a very fitting closing to this article more than twenty years ago:

"My own experience has proven conclusively that maximum results have been obtained through investing in growing companies, keeping these companies until they have completed their growth, and discarding them when the public fancy has changed them into 'blue chips' and pushed them to fantastic heights where they are unattractive because of their ridiculously high price ratio to current earnings.

A good horse can't go on winning races forever, and a good stock eventually passes its peak. Progress is the catch-word of today, so let's forget the old idea of what constitutes a conservative security and climb on the bandwagon with tomorrow's 'blue chips'."

———

ABOUT THE AUTHOR

Richard H. Jenrette is the retired chairman, president, and CEO of The Equitable Companies as well as the co-founder and long-term chairman of Donaldson, Lufkin & Jenrette, the investment banking and securities firm. A former chairman of the Securities Industry Association, he is a member of the New York Society of Security Analysts, the Institute of Chartered Financial Analysts, and is a chartered life underwriter. Mr. Jenrette has been a trustee of the Rockefeller Foundation, the Duke Endowment, and the University of North Carolina, where he received the Distinguished Alumnus Award. He received his MBA from Harvard's Graduate School of Business Administration in 1957. In 1984, he was honored with the Harvard Business School Alumni Achievement Award.